Of Jaguars and Butterflies

Of Jaguars and Butterflies

Metalogues on Issues in Anthropology and Philosophy

Geoffrey Lloyd and Aparecida Vilaça

berghahn
NEW YORK • OXFORD
www.berghahnbooks.com

First published in 2023 by
Berghahn Books
www.berghahnbooks.com

© 2023, 2025 Geoffrey Lloyd and Aparecida Vilaça
First paperback edition published in 2025

All rights reserved. Except for the quotation of short passages
for the purposes of criticism and review, no part of this book
may be reproduced in any form or by any means, electronic or
mechanical, including photocopying, recording, or any information
storage and retrieval system now known or to be invented,
without written permission of the publisher.

Library of Congress Cataloging-in-Publication Data
Names: Lloyd, G. E. R. (Geoffrey Ernest Richard), 1933- author. | Vilaça, Aparecida, 1958- author.
Title: Of jaguars and butterflies : metalogues on issues in anthropology and philosophy / Geoffrey Lloyd and Aparecida Vilaça.
Description: New York : Berghahn Books, 2023. | Includes bibliographical references and index.
Identifiers: LCCN 2022054591 (print) | LCCN 2022054592 (ebook) | ISBN 9781800739048 (hardback) | ISBN 9781800739055 (ebook)
Subjects: LCSH: Philosophical anthropology.
Classification: LCC BD450 .L557 2023 (print) | LCC BD450 (ebook) | DDC
128--dc23/eng/20230221
LC record available at https://lccn.loc.gov/2022054591
LC ebook record available at https://lccn.loc.gov/2022054592

British Library Cataloguing in Publication Data
A catalogue record for this book is available from the British Library

EU GPSR Authorized Representative
LOGOS EUROPE, 9 rue Nicolas Poussin, 17000, LA ROCHELLE, France
Email: Contact@logoseurope.eu

ISBN 978-1-80073-904-8 hardback
ISBN 978-1-83695-081-3 paperback
ISBN 978-1-83695-221-3 epub
ISBN 978-1-80073-905-5 web pdf

https://doi.org/10.3167/9781800739048

To the memory of Paletó and To'o Xak Wa

Contents

Introduction   1

Chapter 1. Are People and Animals Separate Kinds of Beings?   6

Chapter 2. Could Animal–Human Transformations Be Considered as Dreaming or Hallucinating?   12

Chapter 3. Could We Think of Transformations as Metaphoric?   17

Chapter 4. Similarities and Contrasts with Ancient Greece   23

Chapter 5. Are There Complete and Incomplete Transformations?   32

Chapter 6. How Do Things Become Equivalent?   48

Chapter 7. Is Shamanism a Kind of Disease?   54

Chapter 8. Are There Objects without Perspectives?   55

Chapter 9. Why Are Some Animals Unable to Transform?   65

Chapter 10. Do Transformations Need Proof? Are Shamans and Healers Ever Doubted? 68

Chapter 11. Are Transformations Analogous to Miracles? Is It All about Believing? 80

Chapter 12. Is Proof Linked to Literacy? 83

Chapter 13. Could These Transformations Be Compared to Those in Literary Fiction? 88

Chapter 14. Should We Talk about Ontologies When Faced with a World in Flux? 91

Chapter 15. Anthropologists and Philosophers 106

Conclusion 110

References 115
Index 118

Introduction

This book is the outcome of a sustained collaboration between a social anthropologist and a philosopher. The anthropologist (AV) has spent more than thirty years studying the Wari', a people now numbering some four thousand persons living in south-western Brazil. Since they are not well known, a word of introduction is necessary. Until around the mid-1950s their only contacts with non-Indigenous peoples were through warfare. In retaliation for their war expeditions, but mainly because their lands were rich in rubber, they were heavily attacked by whites and two-thirds of their population was exterminated by the mid-1960s, killed either by bullets or by newly introduced diseases. Attempts at 'pacification' were undertaken first by evangelical missionaries from the New Tribes Mission, who lived among them, translated the Bible and set about converting them to Christianity. However, the reaction of the Wari' was distinctive. After some had indeed been converted, still experiencing diseases and deaths they felt disillusioned with the missionaries and several reverted to their traditional beliefs and confidence in their shamans. Since 2001, however, for several reasons, among them the fear of the end of the world suggested by the Al-Qaeda attack on the US (which they watched on TV), most now say they are Christians.

The philosopher (GL) was trained originally as a Classicist. In recent years, however, he has been engaged especially in the comparative study of ancient Greek and Chinese philosophical systems, with a particular focus on the question of the conditions under which fruitful comparison can be undertaken or indeed is possible.

The two of us deal then with very different societies, separated in both space and time, and the nature of the evidence we have with which to study them differs (mostly oral in the one case and written in the other, and this makes an important difference). However, both ancient Greek and Chinese philosophers quite often proposed ideas that seem strikingly counter-intuitive to most modern commentators, some of which bear interesting resemblances to those in modern ethnographic reports. It is precisely the estrangement that these ideas give rise to that has prompted us to juxtapose them in our dialogue. We should, however, warn the reader that we are not attempting a systematic comparison between these different worlds here. Rather, our aim is to move freely between them in order to understand better why they seem so different from what we, who live in modern urban societies, are used to. We should also make clear that the Wari' are not standing in here for all Amazonian Indigenous peoples. Although their life ways and cosmological thoughts are close to those of several other peoples, there are also important differences between very different Amazonian peoples that we do not attempt to account for here.

Bearing those points in mind, we could not ignore that modern Wari', ancient Greeks and Chinese, and we ourselves all face problems that confront every human group that has ever lived: death, disease, madness, misfortune, what constitutes the humanity of those we recognize as fellow humans, how to behave towards other sentient beings, which beings are indeed sentient and hundreds of other similarly challenging issues. Some of these relate to the physical condition of humankind, others to social relations.

At the same time, the answers that have been given to these and other questions have varied hugely. Very different views have been entertained not just on problems of morality, of right and wrong and good and evil, but also on such issues as the proper relationships within different human groups and between whoever counts as humans and other animals. And these views are reflected in divergent patterns of behaviour. In the process, justificatory or merely descriptive stories are recounted that tell of events that may seem utterly incomprehensible to modern Western academic observers. We shall be reporting tales of the transformation of one creature into another, of humans changing into animals and animals into humans. Some relate to the dim and distant past. But others record the experiences of those telling them.

Many of the ways in which such data has been discussed in the past strike the two of us as unsatisfactory. It is still the case, in parts of the academy, that the strange, the paradoxical and the exotic tend to be dismissed as worthy of little attention if not as evidence of human gullibility. Of course it will not do simply to invoke some notion of a primitive mentality, but nor will it do to treat these phenomena as 'mere' myth or metaphor or as stories told to keep the children quiet. Postulating a different world in which these other peoples live also runs the risk of losing the opportunity to probe the similarities, as well as the differences, between them and us moderns, however we locate ourselves. Our twin claims will be first that we can make some, even if not conclusive, progress in understanding this apparent otherness, and secondly that we can ourselves learn from that exploration.

Both claims reflect our conviction that while differences in lived experience are enormous, that should not lead us to underestimate the extent to which the strangeness we diagnose in others can be compared with features of our own modern belief systems and practices. Maybe 'our' strangenesses are different from 'theirs', but they nevertheless pose similar fundamental problems of intelligibility. While in regard to certain phenomena we recognize that errors can be and have been identified, and in that sense progress has been made, there are still vast swathes of experience where we should admit that we flounder. Bizarre, paradoxical, counter-intuitive ideas are to be found in even the most advanced Western modern science and, of course, are prominent in religious faiths that continue to coexist in more, or less, amicable relations with that science. It is foolhardy to generalize over what 'Western modernity' consists in – and we shall find that the same is importantly true of the Wari', as also of ancient Greeks and Chinese.

We shall start with some field notes that were collected in the last thirty years from the Wari' people. How are we to understand stories of the abduction of humans by animals, the transformation of humans into animals and vice versa? Many of these tales come across as frankly fantastical, even, some might think, the products of an overheated imagination. However, the fact that similar stories are also reported from ancient societies and can be paralleled also in modern ones, including our own, allows us, indeed compels us, to broaden the scope of our inquiry. This is to be an investigation not just of one particular Amazonian society, but of how very different societies have posed and resolved issues to do with the fundamental questions that we mentioned at the outset, such as the relation of humans to other animals. We recognize stark paradoxicalities but use them to probe the conditions of mutual comprehensibility. As we proceed, we discover that the very character of the 'understanding' sought and achieved varies according to context in ways that have seldom been given the attention they deserve.

Problems of translation confront us at every turn and in the process we are led to challenge the applicability of some of modernity's standard concepts, notably such dichotomies as that between soul or mind and body, and the notion of nature itself. Faced with what may initially seem strikingly counter-intuitive beliefs and practices, we resist the easy conclusion that they are strictly unintelligible and rather ponder what lessons we ourselves may learn from investigating how others have coped with aspects of our common human predicament, including, indeed, as we have said, the utterly basic problem of understanding others.

We began our conversation when the first outbreaks of the COVID-19 pandemic occurred, and during the successive lockdowns we were confined to limited exchanges by email. But we decided to retain the informal tone with which we conducted these investigations of ours into fundamental issues in anthropology and philosophy. Recognizing that their tentative, exploratory character reflects the open-endedness of the problems discussed, we borrow an expression coined by Gregory Bateson (1972) and call them metalogues.

CHAPTER 1

Are People and Animals Separate Kinds of Beings?

Anthropologist (**A**): I will tell a story I heard from To'o Xak Wa, my Indigenous adopted mother, from the Wari' people, from the state of Rondônia in south-western Brazilian Amazonia, close to the frontier with Bolivia. I was told it during my fieldwork in 2005, when I was living with her and her husband, my adopted father Paletó, in a village by the Guaporé River, named Sagarana. At the time, To'o was around 60 years old and Paletó 70.

I have to introduce the story by explaining that for the Wari', animals of several different species (but not all) – particularly great predators, like the jaguar, and others that are appreciated as prey – see themselves as human beings. They live in houses, have families, do rituals and speak the human language, which is Wari' language. Although during mythic times they could see each other as humans and communicate, in cosmological (or present) times forms have been defined and the regular communication stopped. Even if people and animals see themselves as humans, they do not see each other like that due to their different bodies. That is to say that what it is for a jaguar to see itself as human is not the same as what it is for the Wari' themselves to do so, for we are dealing with different kinds of human, different humanities. The animals' human perspective eventually became opaque to the Indians, except for their shamans. They are gifted with the ability to change form, whereby they can adopt the animals' bodies and vision.

The consequence of this differentiation of bodies in each other's eyes is a differentiation of worlds, meaning that each species sees things differently, although they share the same language. In anthropology we call this 'perspectivism', following the work of the Brazilian anthropologist Eduardo Viveiros de Castro (1998). Indians see jaguars as animals; jaguars see Indians as prey; jaguars, as humans, drink *chicha* (maize beer), but what they see as *chicha* is blood from the Wari' perspective; a tapir's *chicha* is mud; a jaguar's papaya is the Wari''s paca (a rodent); and so on. In the words of Viveiros de Castro (ibid.) there is one same culture but different natures, which led him to refer to 'multinaturalism' in contraposition to our 'multiculturalism'. Whenever we identify an object with some description, we must ask from whose point of view the description applies.

Animals relate to the Wari' either through predation – when they attack in the same way as humans do, that is, with bow and arrows – or through attracting them to their own social group, which means kidnapping them. The Wari' say that animals always want people for themselves, to make them into kin, and that is what the people become even when they are preyed upon. When captured, people begin to share the animal's perspective, meaning that they will see the animals as humans, with a body like their own. On the other hand, they will be seen by their relatives, if they meet them, as animals.

Let me turn to the story now, which I shall recount as it was told to me (see Vilaça 2021b for a longer version).

When To'o Xak Wa was around 5 years old (my guess after she pointed to a child this age to tell me how old she was), one morning, after a row, her mother went to the stream and, while there, was invited by a young man, her sister's son, who called her 'mother', to accompany him fishing at a spot further on, where, he said, there was a lot of fish. The young man carried her on his back for a section of the path. After a time, the mother began to hear familiar voices calling her, saying: 'It's an animal who called you! It's not a Wari'! Look, here's your daughter! She's crying a lot.' The true nephew shouted at the one pretending to be him, whom everyone except for the abducted woman knew to be a jaguar: 'Leave my mother on the ground!' That was when she realized that her supposed nephew had been licking leaves along the path, just like jaguars do. She looked carefully and saw a small length of tail. Because of her kin calling to her insistently, the jaguar-nephew let her go and vanished. According to To'o, the mother was covered in jaguar fur after being carried. When I asked her whether the mother had feared the jaguar, To'o replied: 'She wasn't afraid. It was a *wari*' [a person]!'

A short while later, they went to a festival in another settlement. To'o's father killed a woodpecker and handed it to his wife for her to cook. Unintentionally, To'o's mother touched her mouth with her dirty fingers, swallowing the blood. This made her a commensal of the jaguars, who eat raw food. At night, the mother was in her house, built in the old style without walls. She was sleeping on the stilt palm platform with her daughter To'o in one arm and a nephew in the other, when a jaguar leapt on top of her and dragged her into the forest by her arms, until it bumped into a tree trunk and fled, pursued by the Wari'. She was bleeding heavily and had jaguar claw marks all over her body. They took care of her and treated her with maize smoke, used by the Wari' to drive away what is sometimes called the soul or spirit of the animals, though, as we shall see, it is rather their double. She was healed of her injuries.

Some time later, by now living in another locality, To'o's father killed many capuchin monkeys in the forest. According to To'o, her mother acted as if she already knew what her father had caught and went to the forest to meet him. Seeing the prey, she bit the neck of a monkey, still raw, and drank all the blood. For the Wari', what they see as blood, the jaguar sees as *chicha* (maize beer). She then quickly spat it out. But what To'o and other people saw emerge from her mouth was not blood but leftovers (like porridge lumps) of maize *chicha*. Having become identified with the jaguars, To'o's mother had started to have two bodies simultaneously, fused: one human, the other animal. She was now capable of a very particular kind of translation: rather than substituting one word for another, as our translators do, she transformed one thing into another within her body.

One time, she called her daughters to bathe in the river. There were many small Leporinus fish visibly swimming about. The mother then said to the girls: 'I'm going to fetch insect larvae. Sew up some leaves so we can roast them.' Meanwhile, the mother caught the small fish. Yet when she showed them to her daughters, they were not fish, they were insect larvae. Narrating the event to me, To'o exclaimed: 'The fish all turned into larvae!' On another occasion, To'o went to the forest with her mother and older sister. They made a straw basket and, on the river, caught many Pimelodella, another type of small fish. Their mother swallowed them raw and spat out bits of *patawa* palm beer. On seeing this, people exclaimed: 'They were fish! They all turned into *patawa*!' It was during this period that To'o's mother started to cure sick people, becoming one of the few Wari' women to act as a shaman.

Noticing my interest in these cases, To'o took me to a house neighbouring our own in Sagarana, inhabited by a woman named A'ain Tot of around 60 years, who herself had been abducted by a jaguar in the guise of her mother.

Paletó, To'o and I sat down on the cement floor of her home, in an area with a television at the back. Next to us sat some of the woman's grandchildren, as well as other people who arrived out of curiosity. We chatted politely until I explained to her the episode that I wanted to hear and record. By the time I had placed my small microphone on her clothing and switched on the recorder, quite a lot of people had gathered around us.

When the event happened, A'ain Tot had been around 5 years old (again, my guess). One day, the adults sent the children to the river to fetch water. This was when her mother appeared and called her so they could catch fish in another spot. A'ain went along. She did not know it was a jaguar, since it was exactly like her mother. On the path they encountered fruits from a palm tree, much relished by the Wari', and her mother removed maize from the basket she was carrying for them to eat with the fruit.

Shortly after, a thorn became stuck in A'ain's foot, which her mother pulled out. At this point, the listeners laughed in surprise, marvelling at the jaguar's very human gesture. After walking for a while, A'ain and the mother stopped to sleep. Milk was seeping from the mother's breast because she was feeding a baby at the time. When A'ain was almost asleep, she perceived a man approach. He lay on top of the mother to have sex. A'ain asked: 'Who is this man?' The mother smacked her bottom lightly a few times. Again the listeners laughed, and Paletó explained to me that mothers do this at night when their children awake. The next day, the pair ate the palm fruit and carried on walking, until the girl heard the voice of her older brother calling her. At this moment, the supposed mother said that she was going to defecate and vanished into the forest. Her kin then approached. A'ain's body was covered in jaguar fur, which they cleaned off. At the end of the narrative, I asked whether she had not seen any trace of jaguar in the supposed mother, a bit of tail or something similar (as happened in To'o's account), to which she responded: 'Nothing. It truly was my mother.' After all, the abductor behaved in many ways precisely like a human being: she carried a basket, there was milk oozing from her breasts, a man attempted to copulate with her and she spoke to say she was going off to defecate. At the same time, contact with the abductor led to A'ain's body being covered with jaguar fur, and the jaguar-abductor fled when the mother's kin approached. While several aspects of the story surprised the audience, they did not challenge the veracity of the account, which was to them entirely credible.

According to the Wari', jaguars have *ximixi'*, or 'heart', which means, apart from the organ itself, mind, intelligence and feelings; thus, when an abducted person's kin arrive, the jaguar releases the victim and departs. As To'o explained to me: 'Jaguars are true people', in the moral sense. The same does not apply to tapirs, who when they take someone do not allow the victim to return. However, Paletó and To'o witnessed a rare case of a lad who was abducted by a tapir and returned. According to Paletó's account, one day the young man went to hunt with other men and disappeared. When they searched for him, they found his footprints following tapir tracks and concluded that the tapir had taken him. His kin cried a lot and after some days searching gave up trying to look for him. A long time later, trekking in the forest, some men saw him. He looked like a human except that he had the knees and hands of a tapir. His body was covered in large tapir ticks and he scratched himself constantly. They removed all the ticks and he got better. But like To'o's mother, he began to act strangely. He ate leaves. One time, he brought back a pile of fruits of a kind that the Wari' do not eat, claiming that they were edible. They treated him with maize smoke, and he seemed to get better. 'Only his knees were like those of a tapir', Paletó said. Today, Paletó explained to me at the time, these abductions no longer occur, not because the animals are incapable or have no desire for humans, but because the forest is now distant and young people no longer go there.

CHAPTER 2

Could Animal-Human Transformations Be Considered as Dreaming or Hallucinating?

Philosopher (**P**): Don't they – the Wari' listeners – consider that those people, like To'o's mother and A'ain Tot, who saw jaguars as kin, might in some sense be hallucinating or dreaming, though of course we cannot assume that the Wari' view of those experiences necessarily coincides with our own? Let me tell you a Chinese story that might have some resemblance to the Wari' one. It is also about transformations.

Unlike in ancient Greece, in ancient China we don't get massive tomes devoted to 'the inquiry into nature', even though there is plenty of curiosity, both about the different groups of animals, and about the rules about which are edible, and even when they should be eaten. There are lots of references to transformations, for example of hawks into pigeons, which are sometimes rationalized by modern scholars as based on observations of their migrations: but commentators find it more difficult to explain away such an example as sparrows turning into clams. We get many such examples in the various versions of the so-called treatises on seasonal rules or Monthly Ordinances, one instance of which is to be found in a second-century-BCE text called the *Huainanzi*. Some of the stories relate to dragons and 'mythical' beasts, but the emphasis is in any case not on what the Greeks called the inquiry into nature, so much as on the need to make sure that humans behave correctly and perform the right rituals in every month of the year – and on the ruler's responsibility for their doing so.

So all of that is background to the famous text in the compilation known as the *Zhuangzi* (fourth to second century BCE). This comes in Chapter 2 (in A.C. Graham's 1981 translation of the so-called 'Inner Chapters', though he uses the older transliteration of the purported author's name, that is Chuang-tzu). This is an extraordinary chapter, full of dialogues in which half the time we cannot be certain who is speaking. It deals with everything from notions of what is other and what is the same, different types of speech acts, how humans fail to understand communication and the limits of what can be understood. But just about every single detail in the stories in the chapter has been the subject of furious controversy, with some preferring pretty heavy-duty metaphysical interpretations, and some trying to do without the baggage of a presumed theoretical 'Daoism'. It ends with the widely known story of the butterfly, but first let me give you the immediately preceding dialogue:

> The penumbra asks the shadow: 'just then you were walking, now you stop; just then you were sitting, now you stand. Why don't you make up your mind to do one thing or the other?
>
> 'Is it that there is something on which I depend to be so? And does what I depend on too depend on something else to be so? Would it be that I depend on snake's scales, cicada's wings? How would I recognize why it is so, how would I recognize why it is not so?'

It's relevant to note that earlier in the chapter the very possibility of asserting that something is the case – or equally that it is not – is challenged, though at points it is conceded that we have to 'rely on' certain things being so. Here, at the end of the chapter, even that is thrown into doubt. The 'relying on' allows us to get on with life but makes no commitment to the reality of what is relied on.

Then, finally, we come to the story of how Zhuang Zhou (i.e. Zhuangzi) 'last night dreamed he was a butterfly, spirits soaring he was a butterfly (is it that in showing what he was he suited his own fancy?) and did not know about Zhou. When all of a sudden he awoke he was Zhou with all his wits about him. He does not know whether he is Zhou who dreams he is a butterfly or a butterfly who dreams that he is Zhou.'

But then the chapter ends: 'between Zhou and the butterfly there was necessarily a dividing: just this is what is meant by the transformations of things.'

All of that is more or less Graham's translation. This is contested through and through and the crucial text at the end – which is much disputed – has to be said to be especially opaque. To try to give you more of a flavour of the original, it could be read: 'Suddenly he awoke, suddenly Zhou. He [but we have to supply the subject, for none is given] does not know the dreaming of Zhou makes for [i.e. 'as'] a butterfly? The dreaming of a butterfly makes for [as] Zhou? As regards Zhou and the butterfly, then necessarily there is a separation. This is what is called things' transformation.'

So we are left with butterflies being butterflies, and Zhou Zhou (there is a 'separation of things'), but whether a butterfly is Zhou dreaming he is one, or Zhou is a butterfly dreaming he is Zhou, those are issues over which the text casts radical doubt.

A: Differently from what you report from the *Zhuangzi*, there is nothing about dreaming or hallucinating in the Wari' perception of their stories about transformations. Although they say that people and the animals that are human could manifest themselves in a different shape, related to their double, and that this also happens, among other circumstances, during dreaming, nobody who listened to To'o's story ever considered this transformation as analogous to what happens in a dream, which they talk about in a quite different register. Also, the idea of a clear separation between humans and animals (butterflies in your case), if transposed to the Wari' world, could be thought of as something that is not a given, an a priori thing, but depends on actions. The Wari' used to struggle daily to keep themselves separated from animals. Of course, they do this because they were not separated in the pre-cosmological or mythic world, and that world is always making itself present in their daily lives. This in turn means that the humanity of animals has concrete consequences for the way people live.

P: It might be useful to add that not just the Chinese, but also ancient Greek philosophers had a lot to say about the transformations between humans and animals and those of animal kinds between themselves. Let's go back to what they think about butterflies. Now, the usual Greek term for a butterfly is *psychē*, which is also the term for 'soul' or 'life', and as such was the subject of some pretty intense interest, and not just on the question of whether and if so how it survives after death. Jeremy Mynott, whose *Birds in the Ancient World* (2018) is a very thorough study of more than just birds (for which it is strongly recommended), has pointed out the surprising anomaly that there are in fact virtually no clear references to butterflies in extant Greek literature down to Aristotle, even though there are lots of references of different kinds to living creatures and their behaviour from Homer onwards. One might have expected Homer and the lyric poets to use butterflies to convey the transience of things, but that does not happen. It's more often falling leaves and dying blossoms and the like that get to be invoked.

When we get to Aristotle the picture changes dramatically. In the *Historia Animalium*, Book 5 551a (Mynott (2018: 118) gives a translation), he gives a pretty full description of butterflies' life cycle from caterpillar to chrysalis to fully formed imago. Mynott discusses various speculations as to why we have to wait until Aristotle for this recognition of butterflies, but ends up admitting defeat. The possibility of confusion with the other sense of *psychē* is there, but that did not deter later writers. Nor was Aristotle himself taken aback by this and other examples of what we call metamorphosis, although it presents quite a challenge to his usual confident view that each species of animal has a determinate set form. I would contrast Theophrastus' worrying over the question with regard to plants of whether it is the wild specimen or the cultivated one that gives us access to the *nature* of the species in question – he concluded interestingly that it is the cultivated one that is so, since it is only with cultivation that the plant fulfils its full potential.

As for ordinary Greek peasants, farmers, fishermen, we have no reason to doubt that they were well aware of the changes that frogspawn, for instance, undergoes, and of hundreds of other similar cases. But it has to be said that all that knowledge tends to get drowned out when the natural philosophers, Aristotle in the van, stipulate that each species has its particular form and set of functions, its essence – sometimes pretty clear to observation, as they would claim, but sometimes anything but. However, we can and should remark that both in ancient Greece and among the Wari', it is accepted that what different groups of people 'see' varies. A philosopher of science might say that of course it does, because our observations are always carried out against the background of certain presuppositions concerning what is there to be observed. They are, as the jargon goes, 'theory-laden', although sometimes the 'theories' in question are implicit and so hardly theories at all.

CHAPTER 3

Could We Think of Transformations as Metaphoric?

P: I reckon change and transformation are key topics that enable us to travel from Amazonia to ancient Greece and China and back, even as we stay alert to differences. As I read you, while in Wari' land everything is shifting or liable to shift, some events are more dramatic realizations of this than others. Your remarks about an earlier (greater) ease of transformation suggest to me that transformations as experienced by your interlocutors are recognized as out-of-the-ordinary, harking back to an earlier state of affairs. Jaguars doing some abducting is not exactly everyday, is it? – even though consciousness of the possibility may be universally shared. In which case it might look as if their contrast between ordinary and extraordinary goes some way to mapping on to what since the Greeks we have been used to considering 'natural' versus 'unnatural' (the latter stretching from anomalies all the way to miracles). Is it at all possible to distinguish entities that are particularly liable to transformation from those where that is less likely?

A: The Wari' have a more or less clear-cut list of animals that transform (*jamu* in Wari' language). They say they are *xirak*, meaning 'strange', 'magic'. Sometimes it varies between shamans, but some animals are in every transformation's list: jaguar, peccary, anteater, armadillo, tapir, several species of monkeys (like the capuchin), all fish, snakes. Those are the potentially human animals, meaning not just that they see themselves as human beings and behave accordingly, but that they can be seen as humans by the Wari', mainly the shamans. The only monkey species that does not transform is the spider monkey. The myth says that the members of this species were human, but some of them decided to capture a Wari' woman to marry, and since then they cannot transform any more. *Xirak* covers a wider range of situations. Animals that cause diseases are *xirak*, but witches are also *xirak*, and people that behave badly are *xirak*. Impaired or disabled people are *xirak*. It means abnormal, different. They could be bad or good, depending on their actions.

P: The transforming versus non-transforming contrast cuts across the extraordinary versus ordinary divide insofar as it appears to be normal for some animals but not for other ones to transform (even though there may be different accounts of the list in question). Are all those transforming animals considered edible prey? Is there any correlation with eating restrictions? I recall you reporting the relief the Wari' felt when they realized that the Genesis story they learned from North American evangelical missionaries, who arrived in the 1950s to convert them, gave them licence to eat lots of animals that had been prohibited because they now understood that God had created all of them for the benefit of humans.

A: Ordinary or extraordinary depends on the situation. Let me begin by introducing the pair: true (*iri'*) versus false, strange or not the original one (*kaji*). A stone axe is *iri' kixi* ('our true axe') and a metal axe is *kaji kixi*. When they want to say that I (Aparecida) am a Wari' person, they would say I am *iri' wari'*. The opposite would be *kaji wari'* or *wari' paxi* ('more or less', 'almost' or even 'she is saying so, but she is not really Wari''). The foreign domesticated pig is *kaji mijak* and a peccary is *iri'* *mijak*. To'o, narrating about her mother, said she was *iri' kopakao'* (jaguar). She said so to emphasize that she (To'o) was not playing with us, that what she was telling really happened. *Iri'* with the suffix *o* is also a kind of exclamation mark, like our 'Is that so?' It is a way to say to a person, during a conversation, that you like and approve of what they are saying. '*Iri' o?*' It can also work as a question: 'really?', 'are you sure?'

Getting back to the animals that transform, *jamu*, the Wari' call all of them *iri'* (true) *karawa* ('prey', 'food'), because, except for the jaguar and the snakes, they are their preferred prey. If everything is done correctly, meaning the killing and the preparation of an animal, it will not cause disease, especially if it has been seen by a shaman, who will extract from the animal all of its human attributes (mainly body adornments) and the remains of food. We also have to consider that edibility depends on the state of life. Menstruation, childbearing, war and other critical occasions imply taboos on *iri' karawa* too.

Thus, while the Wari' have plenty of ways of distinguishing true and false and real and fake, they do not have a category that is equivalent to our 'metaphorical', so it would be foolish of us to think that that supplies the key to our understanding of those stories I introduced at the beginning.

P: You said that spider monkeys do not *jamu*. Are spider monkeys never hunted? I am asking whether it is edibility after all that provides the criterion for which animals do and which do not *jamu*. Does that make sense?

A: The Wari' also eat animals that do not *jamu*, like the spider monkey. We could say that animals that *jamu* are the preferred prey not because they transform, but despite that. They taste good so it is okay to take the risk (although, as I pointed out, precautions need to be taken in killing and preparing the animal the right way, so as not to affront it). But I guess there is more to it. Choosing the human animals as preferred prey is a way to keep the multiplicity of perspectives present in the Wari''s daily lives.

P: If animals who are able to transform are those who see themselves as humans, why would this be a 'transformation' at all?

A: In fact, they only transform to external eyes, as they are already humans to themselves. It is all about who is capable of seeing or not. Usually the shamans are. We can say that transformations are all relations. To affirm this you need a third point of view. We do not say that from the jaguar's point of view it transforms. It sees itself always as a human. What varies is if it sees some human as a human too or as prey. So the transformation is in the relationship between the jaguar and the human or prey. It is not one between the jaguar qua jaguar and the jaguar qua human, for from the jaguar perspective it is itself always human. From the Wari' perspective, what they see is a jaguar. But they know (and the shamans can see) that the jaguar sees itself as a human.

P: Turning back to the ancients, the transformations of animals even now in the existing cosmic dispensation (i.e. not just in origin stories) are a very common theme in ancient China even before Buddhist influences came to be prominent. Animals are good to think with, not just as providing paradigms of human behaviour patterns (courage, cunning, deceitfulness) but as exemplifying change and the difficulty of fixing identity. Is Zhuangzi, on waking from dreaming he was a butterfly, really a butterfly now, dreaming he is Zhuangzi? But of course Zhuangzi is in no way a 'typical' author, whatever we might mean by that: he does not represent anybody but himself. But this is useful in querying just how far the contrast between oral and written recording is a key differentiating factor. The author(s) of this Chinese text were clearly highly literate and they show that in their ability to capture the spirit of the oral mode. One of the really striking things about his text is that you can often not be sure who is speaking, and the dramatis personae certainly includes some weird characters.

In Greece we can find the idea of rebirth as another kind of animal or plant in highly literate writers who are assigned important places in the history of philosophy or the history of science (Empedocles for one), and the idea that other creatures arise from the degeneration of humans (actually just males) is there in Plato, no less. So much for the supposition of a sharp divide between 'myth' and mere storytelling on the one hand, and serious philosophy on the other. The idea that how you are reborn reflects your moral character in this life is made much of: but again the use of myth for moral lessons should not surprise us. There are surely what we can recognize as moral implications in the myths Lévi-Strauss collected in his *Introduction to the Science of Mythology* (1970–81). And there are plenty of implicit moral lessons in the folk tales that continue to circulate in every society, however modern and sophisticated it may claim to be.

Surely stories of transgression and its consequences count as such conveyors of values, and surely transgression itself implies the assumption of boundaries to be transgressed. Structuralism would no doubt insist that the units of analysis should be not single myths but concatenations of them. But the point remains that the contrasts between hot and cold, theoretical and concrete science, works of high literature and orality should not be overdone. And quite how each of those pairs is to be construed, whether as mutually exclusive or not, is problematic.

It is true that some of my ancient Greeks are in the business of setting up borders, between proper naturalists and mere fishermen, between those with causal explanations of diseases and those with a battery of empirical remedies. But I suppose I have to recognize that I have spent an inordinate amount of time querying just what was going on then – and now in the way that those borders continue sometimes to be policed. But the theme of transformations gives us a marvellous instance where we can break down some barriers.

A: The well-fixed borders remind me of Latour (1993) and his 'Moderns'. In that case, transformations are seen as abnormalities and are hidden or domesticated (moving to literature, for example, or staying as myth or children's stories). I do not imply that for Amerindians transformations are daily events, but they talk a lot about it and think about it, instead of trying not to see it (by moving transformers to asylums, for example). I agree with you that the phenomenon occurs widely, in the past and in the present, but the way people deal with it tells us a lot. So, the question is not if people transform into animals, but how people view it, don't you think? How much is it part of their lives, talks, concerns, fears, dreams?

CHAPTER 4

Similarities and Contrasts with Ancient Greece

P: I have to emphasize that *some* Greeks set up borders, but not all do! Let me give you a very quick glimpse of the variability of Greek thought.

The history of Greek thought has often, even usually, been told by modern scholars from the point of view of the gradual but assured triumph of Reason. In pre-classical times, we are told, myth and superstition were rampant. From the late sixth or early fifth century BCE, Greek thinkers were seen as relying on reason to insist that (fictitious) myths should be replaced by (rational) *logos*, the term that spans word, story, ratio and rational account. Beliefs that diseases could be caused by gods or demons (*daimones*) were attacked by ancient experts just as much as they have been by more modern ones as superstition (*deisidaimonia*) promulgated by charlatans and quacks who had no idea about the true – natural – causes of diseases and who were exploiting the gullibility of their clientele to make money out of them.

That whole account of progress 'from myth to reason' was grossly superficial, misrepresenting (among other things) the semantics of *muthos* as well as of *logos*, ignoring the ongoing elements of mythologizing that continued in Greek philosophy until the end of pagan antiquity and on into the Christian era, and ignoring also the fact that the writers who accused other healers of charlatanry were often themselves in no position (we would say, that is the positivists would) to give an accurate causal account of diseases or to cure their patients. There was a much more level playing field between 'scientific' and 'traditional' or 'alternative' accounts in Greek antiquity than there is nowadays.

Dodds's (1951) pioneering *The Greeks and the Irrational* did much to undermine earlier positivist accounts of what was called the Greek Enlightenment, though that book itself speculated far too superficially about Greek 'shamans'. Yet although in the wake of Dodds and other studies of Greek religion (Burkert 1972 and Parker 1983 especially) scholars did tone down their more extreme triumphalist statements, the notion that Greek philosophy dispelled the fog of earlier ignorance was still common to most histories. The third volume of Guthrie's (1969) classic *History of Greek Philosophy* was, after all, simply entitled *The Fifth-Century Enlightenment*.

At first sight, quite a bit of the evidence we have for prominent early Greek 'philosophers' – Thales, Pythagoras, Xenophanes, Heraclitus, Empedocles – seems to lend itself to an 'emerging Enlightenment' interpretation. The argument would be that on the one hand you have notable 'scientific', mathematical and astronomical discoveries, such as that the moon shines with light from the sun and that solar eclipses occur when the moon intervenes between the sun and the earth. Yet on the other, there are still stories of 'religious' beliefs, in metempsychosis or the reincarnation of souls in different species of living creatures, and plenty of ritual proscriptions associated with the Pythagoreans especially: 'don't stir the fire with a knife', 'keep your hands from beans', 'don't urinate facing the sun'. In the 'emerging Enlightenment' story the latter are often treated as residues from a more 'magical' period or importations from other ancient Near Eastern cultures (or both).

That second line of argument (foreign influences) is one the ancient Greek sources themselves use often enough, sometimes positively (the Greek appreciation of Eastern wisdom), sometimes negatively (this is where the superstition comes from). Quite a few in the checklist of sages I've just mentioned were said to have travelled to the East and brought back ideas and practices that they incorporated into their own teaching. That applies to Thales and Pythagoras in particular. But that of course left open the question of *why* they picked up the specific ideas they did and indeed wanted to persuade their fellow Greeks of their validity, if, that is, this is what they did (which has been doubted).

Then there have been plenty of ancient and modern attempts to rationalize what is going on in those ritual prohibitions. Thus the interdiction on beans was sometimes taken to have an antidemocratic message, since beans were used as voting counters, though that was only one of five or six attempts to explain and justify it. 'Don't stir the fire with a knife' gets to be glossed (Diogenes Laertius 8.18) as a warning not to stir up the passions or the swelling pride of the mighty (I don't think any ancient author actually points out that if you put a metal blade in a fire it will lose its 'temper' and its edge, which will accordingly have to be restored by reforging).

The trouble is that this combination of 'magic' and 'science' just will not do as an interpretation, short of attributing some kind of split personality to many of these ancient worthies. We are obliged, rather, to adopt the methodological principle that they – the actors themselves – saw no incompatibility between the different elements in their teaching. Take Empedocles, for whom the evidence available to us is particularly rich (though to be sure, far from comprehensive). He is responsible for the first clear statement of what became a key Greek cosmological and physical idea, namely that of the primary elements or ultimate constituents of which everything else is composed. He called them 'roots'. But although he sometimes names these with the ordinary terms for fire, air, water and earth, he also calls them by the names of gods, and this is no mere literary flourish since he clearly holds that they are divine. Now, apart from bits of a book concerning Nature, we also have material associated with a work (or it may be another part of the same book) that relates to *purifications*, which is all to do with how you should look after your soul and how the soul faces reincarnation, whether into another human or an animal or plant. In this, Empedocles tells us that he was himself born as a boy, as a girl, as a bush, a bird and a fish (Diels-Kranz 1952: Fr. 117).

In another excerpt Empedocles tells us that he goes around his home city of Acragas accepted as a god, and people line up to ask for 'the word of healing' for every kind of disease (Diels-Kranz 1952: Fr 112). Now, he does not specify what kind of 'word of healing' that might be, and it might be advice about some medicine or other. However, the word for 'word' here (*baxis*) is also a word for 'oracle', and it is certainly possible that what Empedocles dispensed was one of the charms or incantations that the Hippocratic writer of *On the Sacred Disease* associates with the mumbo jumbo (his word is *deisidaimonia*) of the quacks he labels 'purifiers'. This ambivalence is deeply embedded in Greek medicine. The word for drug (*pharmakon*) is also used for poison and for a (verbal) charm.

So for us moderns to try to drive a wedge between the 'science' and the 'magic' and the 'religion' in Empedocles is to impose our categories quite arbitrarily. Of course, some will still protest that this is early days in the development of science and it cannot be expected to have leapt fully armed from the brow of Empedocles or anyone else. To be sure, there are occasions on which we can draw certain distinctions where modern categories can be applied, *sous reserve*, with caveats. But I would insist that the dangers of distortion are such as to recommend suspending those categories while we investigate the relationships between the different styles, aims and methods that the ancient actors themselves used.

A key challenge for our understanding relates to a belief that looks to have quite a similarity to those that pose problems in the evidence for such a society as the Wari'. I mean the belief that starts from the idea that some species of animals transform into others and leads towards, or at least is connected with, the generalization that all living beings are, in some sense, kin. We have seen Empedocles talk about his reincarnations, and the kinship of all living creatures is represented in sources that date from different epochs as a fundamental tenet of Pythagoras himself. The difference from the Wari' beliefs that you have pointed out is that they (the Wari') speak of transformations during a single lifespan, not just of reincarnations after death. Their transformations are reversible. But the similarity is that these transformations challenge the idea of rigid species boundaries.

Here then we are confronted with beliefs that simply do not make sense to our biology, except that when we investigate evolution, we ourselves, with the benefits of modern science, can and must accept that species are certainly not immutable. Biology says that even though there is evolution, in the normal course of life species of animals usually breed true. There are hybrids, some of which are fertile, others not. But which are and why are questions to be resolved by the analysis of their chromosomes, genes and DNA, not settled a priori. As for how we as humans live our lives, we do not turn into other creatures.

But powerful as a mode of investigation (modern) biology is, it is for sure not the only discourse about living beings that can and should inform the answer to that question of how we should behave. Nor has biology itself got to the bottom of the question of consciousness, of which sentient creatures can and do feel anything like we feel, whether it be pain or pleasure or any other experience that rates as phenomenal consciousness.

Some will arrive at some conclusions concerning how we should relate to animals of various kinds by pondering their own direct experiences, whether that be of domesticated species or of the wild ones they may encounter (and these will not be many in the lives of the majority of urbanized humans). But the evidence and the arguments with which to try to build up universally valid recommendations just are not there: *universal* recommendations are a mirage.

The takeaway lesson, then, is obvious enough. We cannot be satisfied with the view that the sciences have a monopoly of important truth. Biology in my example is not the only discourse we should attend to. In point of fact, few people spend most of their time engaged in that discourse. But then it is not the case that many attend to what the poets have to say on the subject of other living creatures either. This remains generally true despite the popularity of the work of Ted Hughes, for instance, whose marvellously sensitive poems break down the barriers between the human-like behaviour of birds, such as the crow, and the animal-like behaviour of humans (Hughes 1970). But as for what we should attend to, when we do attend to it, we have to admit that there is no overriding authority we can turn to for the answers.

At this point, positivist historians of science might be prepared to make a few minor concessions but not retreat from the major claim that Greek philosophy and science indeed represented a triumph of reason, as I put it. Of course – the concessions might go – many of the most important figures in the story of the Great Geniuses in the history of science, Thales, Empedocles, even Archimedes, were complex personalities, and that continues to be the case with most of the Geniuses of the scientific revolution, Galileo, Kepler, Newton, down to the physicists of the last two centuries. Of course talk of a Greek 'miracle' – they might further concede – strikes the wrong note. Yet those admissions, they will argue, do not affect the principal point, that the inquiry into nature represents a fundamental breakthrough, the rejection of many traditional superstitious ideas and practices and the adherence to a new methodology of how to go about investigating natural phenomena. Where magic and ritual are never progressive, once the inquiry into nature got going, progress, the advance of knowledge, could be sustained (even if it often was not), helped, of course, by the rise of literacy, conserving earlier ideas and making them available to scrutiny.

The work of interpreting and evaluating the leading figures in the story of Greek science, from Thales and Empedocles through Plato and Aristotle and Euclid and Archimedes and onwards, is ongoing. But what the positivist story still leaves out of account is first that the success of reason is never complete, and secondly that in its presumed onward and upward march a good deal is lost at the same time as much is gained. Thus, on the first score, pretty well all of the key figures had their more or less (often less) conventional views about the divine – for most of the ancient ones the heavenly bodies were gods, whether or not they further held that the stars influenced the fortunes of humans on earth.

But maybe the second of my two points is the more important one, namely the potential downside of the advance of rational explanations of natural phenomena. The best example of this may be the theme of purifications. I have noted how some of the Hippocratic doctors were contemptuous of the claims of those they labelled 'purifiers', who claimed to be able to diagnose which divinity was responsible for which complaint and to provide remedies in the form of charms and incantations. To be sure, we cannot now access what the fifth-century 'purifiers' themselves might say in their own defence (unless we count Empedocles as one of them), but we do have extensive evidence from the second century of our era relevant to the problem. This is in the so-called *Sacred Tales* of the orator Aelius Aristides (Behr 1968), a great advocate of the powers of Asclepius, whom he describes as his Saviour, and this despite the fact that no sooner was Aelius cured of one terrible ailment than he succumbed to another. However, throughout his ghastly disease-ridden life his faith in what we call temple medicine remained unshaken, and he repeatedly contrasts the skills of ordinary doctors unfavourably with those of Asclepius himself.

What then are we to make of this? Drawing on the distinction between 'efficacy' and 'felicity', we may observe that even though Aelius continues to have a terrible health record he evidently takes considerable comfort from his conviction that the god is there to help him. The successes of temple medicine could then be said to lie more in the psychological support they offered than in the perceived efficacy of the remedies suggested, even though it is efficacy that was often claimed by the advocates of that style of medicine. They wanted cures, not just reassurance. We should register that at no stage in Greco-Roman antiquity was temple medicine put out of business by those who considered it mere superstition. To repeat my earlier point, if we stick to the discourse of biomedicine, appeals to divine intervention are simply irrelevant to the patients' recovery. But if we admit that that is not the only discourse in play, then we may allow space for the therapy of the word. Indeed, that continues to bulk large in the treatments that modern psychiatry relies on, even while psychiatry itself has to acknowledge that it is often in no position to secure the health of its patients (which corresponds to my first point, to do with the incomplete triumph of rationality).

Where does this leave us? No one could maintain that the ancient Greeks throw up no problems of the deeply challenging kind that we encounter among the Wari'. Earlier certainties concerning the sustained onward progress of science cannot be maintained. The problems we face of distinguishing plain mistakes from differences in perspective are not to be resolved by some handwaving towards generalizations about rationality. Those problems have to be treated seriatim, one by one. But some of them can be: sometimes we are in a position, guided by our sources, to undertake some interpretation. Yet when we investigate the criteria we invoke to arrive at such judgements, we have to recognize those different discourses that I have spoken about. Different discourses seem important to different groups. Some that take centre stage for modernity do not and did not preoccupy other peoples now and at other times. But we have to observe how short-sighted modernity is proving to be. We rely on it often, rather than on alternatives. But there has to be a question mark over just how well based that reliance is. For sure there should be room for other voices.

CHAPTER 5

Are There Complete and Incomplete Transformations?

P: Let's go back to your stories. To'o told you about the capuchin monkey hunt, where her mother bites the neck of a monkey and then spits out its blood. You go on, 'but what To'o and other people saw emerge from her mouth was not blood but leftovers of maize *chicha* (beer). For the Wari', what they see as blood, the jaguar sees as *chicha*.' But that surprised me. For you had just said that To'o and others saw what her mother spat out as leftovers of *chicha*. But that would be a jaguar perception, would it not? I would have expected you to say that what To'o and others saw would be blood and it would only be To'o's mother who would have said – in her jaguar body mode – that what she spat out was *chicha*.

A: Her mother was playing with perspectives as a shaman-to-be (she became a shaman afterwards), for whom perspectives used to mix sometimes. She was a jaguar but also a human, having a double perspective. Our expectation might be that any given individual has only one perspective at a time. But for the Wari' that is not the case, as we can see from this example of a shaman being in a sense a double being. More generally, indeed, as Eduardo Viveiros de Castro has already pointed out, the character, shape or identity of almost everything in their world is dependent on actual relations. We can compare what is true of kinship positions for us: a woman would be a daughter from her mother's point of view, but will also be a wife, sister or aunt from other perspectives, and each of those roles will imply different obligations, pressures and perceptions.

Answering your question, from the beginning to the end of the action, To'o's mum saw *chicha* and not blood. To'o and the others also saw *chicha*, although they inferred that it was blood, as it came out of her mouth after she bit the raw monkey. The Wari' might put it that the mother made it look like *chicha* to the others after making it (the blood) pass through her body, in which case we might say that her body acted as some kind of translating machine.

P: Obviously this question of double bodies is a crux, as also is the idea of the body as a translation machine. But for now may I concentrate on a different point? Your story seems to imply that there are incomplete versus complete transformations. So, how do the jaguars present themselves when embarking on an abduction? In the case you described, To'o's mother is invited fishing by someone who looks just like her nephew. When the true nephew calls out, To'o's mother looks carefully and sees a small length of tail. But having been carried by the nephew-jaguar she was covered in jaguar fur, which she could not see as such, though until the very end she was not frightened because the jaguar was a *wari'*. Similarly, in A'ain Tot's abduction scene that you describe, where there is another case of a body being covered in jaguar fur, you asked whether there had been any trace of jaguar in the supposed mother, a bit of tail, for instance, to which you get the reply, 'Nothing. It truly was my mother.'

One question this prompts is whether the expectation is that the jaguar-abductor completely transforms into human shape or not. The first of those two cases suggests not (the length of tail is the giveaway), but the second reports that there were no residual traces of jaguar (no trace of a tail). And it seems that it is not only the jaguar-abductor that can be in a bit of an in-between or hybrid state. At least the effects on their victims (bodies covered in jaguar fur) are only temporary or can at any rate be remedied. For the kin in that second case succeeded in cleaning off the jaguar fur. But one thing that emerges pretty clearly is a preoccupation with, and uncertainty about, personhood, that is the perspective from which the agent is seeing things.

A: I wouldn't say that the transformations are incomplete, but that there is always more than one perspective in play and they slip from one to the other. On the body appearance of the jaguar-abductor, experiences vary. Some people told me that they are totally human, others could see some traces of animality after their perspectives began to change, when they heard their true relatives' voices. This is also a way to explain to me that the situation involves perspectives in motion, not fixed ones. What we have are visions that move from one kind of body to another. You have also to consider that, of course, the answer that To'o gave to me, stating that her mother could see a jaguar's tail, was a reaction to my question. It is as if she wanted to say that yes, by the end her mother, after connecting again with her true relatives, was not sharing the jaguar's perspective any more.

P: In the case described, the dramatis personae include To'o's mum (TM), To'o (T), the jaguar (J) and you (A). There seems to be no doubt that TM recognized the monkeys that her husband had shot as monkeys.

A: Yes, she did. But at the same time they could easily have added that she was thirsty, longing for *chicha*, which was the monkey's blood.

P: You go on to say that according to T, her mother (TM) drank the blood of a monkey, and quickly spat it out. What is the 'it'?

A: She spat out the blood, which was equivalent to *chicha*, as TM made the translation through her body, which, as I said, was a double one, meaning a body with a double perspective, as shaman's bodies are.

P: You go on that, still according to T, what she and others saw was not blood but leftovers of *chicha*. You then make the remark that what the Wari' see as blood, the jaguar sees as *chicha*, and then elaborate your next point, that TM has a double body, both human (where the blood is blood) and jaguar (where it is *chicha*). I take it that it is you (A) speaking here as the anthropologist-observer. When T says to you that the blood was spat as *chicha* leftovers, do you think she is giving you, the anthropologist, a gloss on what had happened herself? Was T in fact acting as intermediary commentator to give you her own and the Wari' point of view, namely that the Wari' allow that where they see blood, jaguars see *chicha*? But then why would T have glossed what came out of her mum's mouth as leftovers of *chicha*? If T and the other bystanders saw *chicha* coming from TM's mouth, does that not mean that they, the bystanders, or at least T herself, were beginning to share a jaguar point of view?

A: That is a very interesting question. If things followed a strict logic, it should have been like you said. But they didn't. To'o herself did not explain much about that point. She was telling me about how odd her mother was. At that point they did not know that she was turning into a shaman. Everything was a bit blurred. She just told me that her mother oddly became very fond of blood and that is why she ran to the raw prey. When they finally saw her spitting *chicha* (in fact, leftovers of *chicha*, meaning that the *chicha* itself had gone), they began to understand that she was taking blood as *chicha*, as if saying that they were both (the mother and the others) humans, who appreciate *chicha*, but different kinds of humans. How the different objects relate, when a shaman is healing someone, is a point worth considering. He (shamans are mainly men) usually sucks the person's body and takes from it some object that nobody else could see as it really is. He says 'look at the arrow', and what you see is a stick. He is translating by words the equivalence between objects. TM was translating through her body, maybe, and that is a good point, because she was still in a process of transition to have a stable animal double, a relatively stable one, that is. There is also an important detail to be considered. T was not sharing the jaguar's point of view in general, but her mother's point of view, which is different. Being a close relative, she has access to her mother's vision, as she still sees her as her mother. We could say that sharing someone's vision is a sign of the closeness of your relationship to them, and that applies not just to other humans but also to animals.

P: Conversely, in the reply T gives you about whether her mum was frightened, TM is reported (by T) not to have been so, since it – the jaguar – was a *wari'*, which you gloss here as 'a person'. Presumably only Wari' count as persons, so this looks like another instance of incomplete or hybrid identification (or am I talking nonsense?).

A: T was saying that it was *wari'* in order to differentiate it from a jaguar. That is the only reason. On other occasions she would definitely say that jaguars are not *wari'*. It all depends on the context of the conversations. It is not a question of incomplete or complete identification, but of emphasis in conversation, here one of T trying to make herself clear to me.

P: T was obviously telling it how it was both for her mum and for herself (she wasn't telling you dreams or hallucinations, I understand). But the question that now lurks is: if you had been there, what would you have seen and what would your friends have expected you to see, given that being adopted by a Wari' family, you had become a Wari', even with a *wijam* (enemy, white) past? The anthropologist's dilemma?

A: Regarding what they would have expected me to see if I had been there, I guess it would be the same as themselves. They would definitely situate me, in such an occasion, at the human or *wari'* point of view. They would be very suspicious of me if I saw just blood. If that had been the case, I would definitely be situated as a *wijam* (enemy) or jaguar and they might be afraid of me, especially because I do not have the same kinship links as TM with T and the rest. I am sure I would have seen blood myself, so I would be in trouble if I said that out loud. But I think the important point is not related to single objects but the passage from one to the other. Except for TM (who just saw *chicha* everywhere), they all saw blood becoming *chicha*. The becoming is much more important than the *chicha* or the blood. Like when fish turned into larvae in the continuation of her story.

P: It's a bit different for an ancient historian. I come to understand and respect others' views and ways of life, but I am not challenged directly to subscribe to them or not. I am not at all sure how far your exchanges with your interlocutors brought to light differences in ontological assumptions between you. A delicate issue for sure. But presumably, in their dealings with the missionaries the Wari' often registered such differences, for unlike you the missionaries were bent on converting them.

A: As an anthropologist I try to just let them speak, without interfering. I know things look strange to me, but I usually do not express my point of view, although it comes out through my naive questions, of course. The Wari' do know I do not share their point of view (at least regarding many issues), that I do not see things as they do, but that I am interested in learning, that I pay attention, respect. That is what the evangelical missionaries do not do. They are explicit about their differences and express it by criticizing. The Wari' used to say that if I stayed even longer there, or better, if I married there, I would definitely share their point of view completely.

P: The residual tails in the stories of abduction do help me, for they underscore the point that there are what I called those incomplete transformations, evidently important when shamans are following the animals and becoming one, but are still able to return to give their advice to their fellow Wari'. But it is striking that when you ask whether there was a residual trace of jaguar, the reply you get is an emphatic nothing. This jaguar-human was not just 'exactly like' the mother, but 'truly' was the mother. But when the elder brother called out, the mother-jaguar vanished into the forest – which I take it means it reverted to jaguarhood. You told me earlier, however, that at some point in her life as a shaman, TM gave up following jaguars to follow capuchin monkeys and later agoutis.

A: As I said, I don't think we could talk about incomplete transformations. Even the shamans are not incomplete, but unstable, double, and that is why a glimpse of the animal body could be seen in his human body. It is as if sometimes a short circuit (my image, not the Wari''s) happens and the bodies and visions mix up. My jaguar grandfather, Orowam, used to make jaguar sounds at night, sleeping at his house with his wife (the human one). She used to tell me this, laughing. It was like the jaguar's tail, a mixture of bodies. In the reported jaguar's case, the focus of the instability they want to stress (concerning the jaguar's tail) is not that of the jaguar's body but of the abducted child, who was becoming a real person (kin of her kin) again, rather than someone who is becoming a jaguar herself. That is what the remark about the tail was meant to say. Before the kin's arrival, the jaguar had no tail, meaning that the child could not see it, as she was totally inside the jaguar's perspective.

P: I must insist on it. As you already told me, the Wari' have a term meaning 'complete': *pin*. I guess it suggests that whether the transformation may or may not be complete is a matter that Wari' register as important. We don't have a specialized locution to deal with that, do we? This might look like a nod to linguistic determinism: Wari' language, at least grammar and syntax, dictates aspects of their vision of the world or even their world itself. But I would counter that it is nothing more than the obvious point that the natural language available prompts (but that does not mean that it necessitates) certain saliences. The point is very familiar from discussions of the vocabulary available for hues.

A: Completeness (*pin*) and, on the other hand, the sense of more or less (*paxi*) are interesting points, although they do not have exactly the same referents as our terms. Sometimes they use them to emphasize a statement, even if it does not involve completeness. Like: *wijam* (enemy) *pin ma*? 'Are you completely enemy?' or 'Have you become completely enemy?' (as they once told me when I forgot a Wari' word when talking to them). Or they could say: *wari' paxi ma*. 'You are not a real Wari'. You are more or less Wari'. We thought you were Wari' but you are not so.'

They also use *paxi* regarding kinship. We begin with the term for kin: *nari*. And you have real kin (genealogical close kin or real affines), glossed as *iri' nari*; the others are 'more or less' kin, *nari paxi*. Paletó, who adopted me, would say that the two of us are *iri' nari*, not *nari paxi*. He does this to make clear that we are related. On other occasions he might have said to his people that I and he are *nari paxi* (if he were angry at me for some reason), or even that we are not kin at all, meaning that I am a *wijam*, enemy. When they say this with respect to animal transformations, they emphasize the strangeness of the event. Like the woman talking about the jaguar who became like her mother. Her words were: *Na'* (my mother; the glottal occlusion

(') is phonemic, meaning that it differentiates words) *pin* (completely) *na* (it/she/he, referring to the transformed jaguar), *iri'* (truly) *na'* (my mother). It was completely my mother, truly my mother. The fact that To'o's mum noted a tail afterwards does not mean that the transformation was incomplete, but that her (the narrator's) vision changed during the event.

P: Your comments on *pin* are okay – it's only to be expected that its use varies and there is not necessarily any background assumption about processes of becoming (though when you say the interest is on the difference between a real jaguar and a fake, I would be intrigued to know how they pick out fakes, i.e. the antonym of *pin*).

A: A fake jaguar is *kaji kopakao'*, which is what they call domestic cats. Nothing to do with jaguar-transforming people.

P: All this discussion complicates the picture interestingly and raises a new difficulty that I had not spotted before. Take a scene with a jaguar, your adopted grandfather, the jaguar-shaman Orowam, another Wari' – say your father Paletó – and you, where what you and Paletó see is a jaguar drinking the blood of a prey it has just killed. What the jaguar itself sees is itself drinking beer. What Orowam sees when he 'jaguarizes' is the jaguar drinking beer, too, presumably, for Orowam now has jaguar eyes. But is it the case that the jaguar can transform into a Wari'? That would mean the jaguar having human eyes. But then it would see the drink as blood, would it not? Or do animals, when they transform into what we see as humans, see themselves as transforming into their prey – in which case they are no longer human, at least for a time? Is this when animals cause human sickness?

A: I think the point we are struggling over on transformations is about the reality of them. In fact, all you have are relations. The jaguar sees itself as human. Then it approaches a human, like Orowam (who in fact became a jaguar-shaman because he was attracted by his father, who himself became a jaguar because he died eaten by a jaguar). Initially the jaguar sees Orowam as a person and wants him as company. Then it makes him ill, cures him and he then becomes a jaguar-shaman. Sometimes the jaguar just sees a Wari' as a prey, an animal. It all depends on the relation the animal establishes with the Wari'. Being attacked by an animal always has a sickness or death as an outcome. Answering your specific question, Orowam will always see jaguars as persons and he may or may not see the blood the jaguar is drinking as *chicha*. It will depend on how he is positioning himself, on the Wari' side or on the jaguar's side. He can see both.

P: What I take away from this is the following. 'Transformation' is not so much something that happens to the body of a creature such as a jaguar, for the jaguar always has the body that it has. Yet my first problem here is that I thought there were cases where the jaguar's body did change. Or was all that happened just a question of what the human observer saw? I am thinking of occasions when the question arises of whether what looked like a human had a jaguar tail, was furry or whatever. The case of To'o's mother is particularly striking. When she had been carried by the jaguar-nephew, her body became covered in fur, and as you put it a little later, she began to have two bodies simultaneously. So here it is not just a matter of perceptions, vision, having certain (types of) eyes, but (also) one of what we would call physical changes (though whether that captures having two different bodies at once looks pretty difficult). But a further question in this set of stories is indeed that of the different perceptions of the agents in question. The true nephew and everyone else witnessing the scene – except the abducted woman herself – knew the imposter to be a jaguar. Yet you do not resolve the situation by saying that it really was a jaguar. Rather, in the continuation To'o said that her mother was not afraid because it was a *wari'* (person). That neatly shows that To'o's mother herself is now in the jaguar position (where other jaguars are humans), but is there not still a difference between her and other jaguars? She has further adventures, but after being mauled by a jaguar she is healed of her injuries and returns to Wari' society, now as a shaman. At the same time, as you recount it, from To'o herself this seems more than just a story of how her mother became a shaman, her *rite de passage*, for To'o endorses the account of the transformations of her mother's body. So this is more than a story of a change in relationship or perspective, but indeed a metamorphosis, which is where I am still rather at a loss. I am not out of the woods (or the forest) quite yet.

A: Your argument is very important. It is not easy to talk about it, maybe because we do not have an adequate vocabulary. First of all, I have to say that usually we take the 'body' as a given object, easily translatable and understandable by any culture. But what I am translating here as 'body' is a concept as complicated as 'soul' is for us. The Wari' name for body is *kwerexi'* ('our body'). Although it includes what we understand as the body, meaning flesh, bones and organs, it also means intelligence, skills, thought, feelings, desires, habits, which, as I've already said, are part of the heart (*ximixi'*), itself a component of the body. Beings who share habits, like those who share food, walk together in the forest or sleep together, end up having similar bodies. That is what happens with couples after marriage, when a person is kidnapped or when shamans walk and hunt with their fellow animals. When generalizing, the Wari' used to say: *je kwerexi' pain ka wari' nexi* ('our – Wari' – body is like that'). This is meant to explain that they, as a group, have some distinct habits or behaviour. There is also an extra complexity to be added to this, as we know that the double, *jamixi'*, manifests itself as another body, also with flesh, bones and intelligence. In a certain sense, it means that among the Wari', we just have bodies everywhere, whose shapes vary according to the relational context, meaning according to the perspectives of the external observers. In the case of To'o's mother, she saw the jaguar as a human with a body similar to hers; her real relatives, on the other hand, saw (or figured out) the jaguar as an animal. The Wari' would say that To'o's mum saw the jaguar's *jamixi'*, while they themselves saw the jaguar's *kwerexi'* (body).

Now, let me explain how I listened to this story when I was there. As an anthropologist I was fascinated, of course. I tried not to ask questions so as not to interrupt the narrative. There were also many Wari' listening by my side. They were all more interested in the actions of the jaguar-mother (cuddling the child in order to have sex with the incoming partner in peace, for example) than with the bodily characteristics of those involved. I followed them, because unlike me they asked many questions during the narrative. What I grasped was that yes, there was a body change, but we should not consider any one unit, but rather the pairs they form. It is not the jaguar itself that is changing but the pair of jaguar-mother and daughter. The kidnapped person saw the tail only when she listened to her real relatives calling her. She did not see the tail before that: the jaguar was a *wari'*, a real (*iri'*) one. It was a fake one, a pretend one, from the Wari' point of view, of course. They would say it was *wari' paxi*, more or less. Like those gestalt pictures where you see one thing or the other and switch between them. The way the kidnapped person had to explain it was by referring to a change in the mother's body (the jaguar's). When To'o's mother was back home and taking care of her children, being a jaguar was only a virtual possibility. She has no jaguar's body, although sometimes they say that a shaman could have a second body acting while their Wari' body is still there among their kin. That is why I do not translate the Wari' concept of *jamixi'* as 'soul' or 'spirit', as it is not something that is there, a part of the self, as it is for (some of) us. It is a potential alter-body, a double, which could come into existence through another person's eyes. Well, when To'o saw her mother running to the father's prey to drink blood, she did not see her body with fur, but a strange behaviour, which is part of the jaguar's body, considering the extended definition of the body I just gave you. When the kidnapped person had fur on her body, it was evidence that people saw that the person was affected by the jaguar, meaning that she was becoming a jaguar. As you see, there are always pairs or groups, not single persons. If the jaguar had succeeded in taking her away, To'o's mum would not be conscious of what had happened to her, first of all because she would never have come back home. Instead, she would have become a jaguar herself and lived with the jaguars as humans. For her Wari' relatives, she would be dead.

P: This exchange between us suggests to me that some of the problems in understanding these transformations may stem from our use of the word 'body', with its associations with the implied contrast with 'soul'. You point out the range in the key Wari' term *kwerexi'*. You pointed out that it does not just include concrete physical flesh, bones and organs. It might refer to intelligence, feelings, habits, behaviour. Of course, we can far more readily understand how a single person can exhibit radically different patterns of behaviour than we can make sense of saying that a single person has two bodies. In your stories it is often the behaviour that is the focus of attention: acting strangely, for instance licking leaves or eating food that should not be eaten. On such occasions, is it not potentially misleading to gloss what is going on by saying that the body of the person concerned is undergoing a physical change?

Let me add that in your comments on *kwerexi'* you talk quite a bit about how the heart fits in, and in that instance our understanding is helped by the fact that in vernacular English too, 'heart' is sometimes the physical organ and sometimes a matter of feelings (and so of behaviour). Could we not say that the expression you quote, *je kwerexi' pain ka wari' nexi*, referring to their collective practices and habits, is just their way of referring to those practices, but does not reduce them to what we call the body? Of course we too sometimes explain behaviour in terms of physical characteristics, as when people are said to be hot-tempered or used to be diagnosed as phlegmatic or melancholic. But when Wari' talk of transformations, is it necessary to see them being committed to more than behavioural ones? Over to you.

A: That is something important to clear up. I still prefer to call it 'body' and will tell you my reasons. The first one is to allow it to be easily compared with our own concept through allowing what you call a semantic stretch. Or by clear contrast between us (moderns) and them (the Wari'). But the main reason to keep the word is because the Wari' never discard the shape, the physical features, exactly what we call the body. A change in habits could not be separated from a change in shape. That is why the kidnapped mum saw a tail (as the jaguar was becoming a jaguar again, reverting to its jaguar's body in the woman's eyes, although not to itself, as the self-perception of shape did not change). Behaviour is shape, form, blood, meat. So, it is different from what it is for us. Calling the Wari' body 'behaviour' will make us lose sight of the difference between them and us (urban Euro-Americans), which is so central to understand them.

P: This issue of the translation of *kwerexi'* carries an important implication for the kind of study we are engaged in here. You prefer the rendering 'body' for the reasons you give. At the same time you point out emphatically that the Wari' term also covers intelligence, personality, behaviour, even perspectives. So no single English word will be fully satisfactory. But this untranslatability does not imply unintelligibility. Rather the key lesson for us to draw is not to reduce Wari' conceptual categories to ours. Theirs, indeed, offer us the opportunity to reflect critically on our own.

A: That is an important remark.

P: If I am allowed to carry my statement of one aspect of my difficulty further, the problem can be stated like this. Ordinarily when the jaguars are going about their business, hunting or whatever, in the jungle, they see themselves as humans. Right? But as humans they would see jaguars as jaguars.

A: They would see their fellow jaguars as humans too. They will refer to them (they speak the same language as the Wari') as *wari'*, human beings.

P: This may be the crucial point. The jaguars do *not* see other jaguars as jaguars (even though human onlookers do just that: for humans, jaguars are jaguars – though there is the possibility, is there not, that this is a shaman-jaguar?). Seeing themselves and their fellow jaguars as humans means that for jaguars, jaguar society is just like human society. The Wari' have this (had this?) on the authority of shamans who have joined jaguar society and can vouch for it. But jaguars, when they encounter humans (I mean human humans, not their fellow jaguars), can either treat those humans as prey to be devoured or as possible companions. Again, presumably the Wari' accept this on the basis of what their shamans report, and I take it that ordinary Wari' entertain the possibility of shaman-like experiences that they themselves might have. All right?

A: That is one way to put it. In fact, treating the Wari' as prey or as possible companions does not present itself as an option given to jaguars, insofar as they are two views on the same action. Jaguar-shamans used to say that when a person suffers a jaguar's attack (from a visible animal), in fact (in the shaman's eyes and the eyes of the jaguar itself) the jaguar is a person acting as a hunter, with bow and arrows. As the outcome is always the killed person becoming part of the jaguar's society, they could say that the jaguars attack not to eat, but to make people over to themselves, to make kin. Preying, from the point of view of animal predators, is companion-making. Every event has several possible explanations that do not exclude one another.

CHAPTER 6

How Do Things Become Equivalent?

P: Here we go again, and this time too it gets into some tricky linguistic issues. You write that maize *chicha* is blood for the jaguar and mud for the tapir. Call this A.

I expected blood to be *chicha* for the jaguar and mud to be *chicha* for the tapir. Call this B.

In a very loose sense these are equivalent, in which case we may say that it does not matter which item is in the subject and which in the predicate position. Or does it? Do your reports allow for what the jaguar thinks about the human perspective? You have lots of lovely examples of what the Wari' think, indeed know, about the jaguar's perspective (as in B, where 'blood' is human-perspective talk, '*chicha*' jaguar's). But does the issue of what the jaguar sees when it sees humans drink *chicha* crop up (as one reading of A would suggest)?

A: The ambivalence was my fault. As you said, there is a linguistic issue here. The Wari' express themselves regarding the jaguar's view like this (and the same applies to other animals or to other peoples). They would say: *Tokwa nain wik, kopakao'*. *Tokwa* means *chicha*; *nain* is *na*, the third-person singular pronoun + *in*, the neutral mark (he/she to it); *wik* is blood; *kopakao'* is jaguar. The translation is: 'the jaguar refers to blood as *chicha*'.

In the beginning of the sentence, *tokwa* is a vocative: '*Chicha*! regarding the blood, says the jaguar.'

You can say the same of kinship terms: *Te inon* Paletó. *Te* is the vocative for father; *inon* is first-person singular pronoun (*ina*) + *on*, the masculine mark: 'I call Paletó father' or 'I say father when referring to Paletó'. The complement is: *Arain na pa'* Paletó. *Arain* is child; *na* is the third-person singular pronoun (he, Paletó); *pa'* is the reflexive, 'to me'. 'Paletó calls myself kid.' If someone asks me: 'are you relatives?' I can answer either that I call him dad or that he calls me kid or daughter.

On the animal's perspective on the Wari', sometimes they elaborate it, sometimes not. Usually this kind of reverse perspective is elaborated when someone is narrating an event, or a myth, which involves the actions of a human-animal regarding a person. But usually the animal's perspective is just a visual issue: you know that the jaguar sees blood as *chicha* because it drinks blood. They do not go further, like the way they do regarding the Wari' perspective on the jaguar. But they know that the jaguars know how the Wari' see the world. Some myths from other Indigenous peoples that were included in Lévi-Strauss's *Introduction to the Science of Mythology* make this point. The animal that kidnaps a human tries to avoid, for example, that the human drinks ayahuasca while living among them, because if the human does, they will see the animals as animals and not as people any more. This is the case with the anaconda in the myths of the Panoan people. From my knowledge, there is no similar myth among the Wari'.

P: What prompts the development of such a notion that A may be 'equivalent' to B? Where lies the boundary between those cases where that is possible, and those where it is unthinkable that a given A could be substituted for a given B? The underlying question I am driving at is the difference between common or garden communications and understandings (where there is little or no doubt about what is going on) and occasions when really important issues, maybe to do with hidden powers and influences, are at stake. We all try to make sense of experience, while entertaining different ideas both about what that experience consists of and what would count as 'making sense' of it. The Kopenawa and Albert (2013) book you gave me shows that Kopenawa had a very clear idea of the answers to those questions, and I reckon from what you say that Paletó did too. We move from an anthropology of peoples to an anthropology of anthropologists. The members of anthropology departments, or departments of HPS (History and Philosophy of Science) come to that, have no monopoly on articulateness on the topic, though we are not renowned for our humility.

A: On the equivalence between A and B, we could say that the Wari' have a kind of 'multispecies dictionary' regarding certain items. So, they all know that blood is *chicha* for the jaguar and mud is *chicha* for the tapir. This is because many stories and myths talk about this, making clear the equivalence. It is also well known that our paca (a rodent) is a papaya for the jaguar. Other items are stuff for discussions and lucubrations. They rely on the stories told by the elders, who do not have a formalized knowledge, but experiences. It is from the reported experiences and myths (taken as remote experiences) that they construct this equivalence. However, all is unstable and can change depending on further experiences (which today, given that they are Christians, do not happen any more, so they always revert to the past experiences). A could be B regarding a specific experience, but may be C regarding another. A kidnapped person will learn new equivalences during the time they spent with the animal. From the reports I've heard, the audience always seems to be surprised by new ones. Oh, so that is it! they used to say.

The point is that they never found it necessary to formalize this knowledge, they keep it fluctuating, they put all the emphasis on the particular experience, the details, the feelings and visions of the narrator. It is a floating knowledge, and things may match each other or not. If not, they would say: oh, that (specific) jaguar is odd!

P: Is there a difference between 'to be' as an essence and 'to be' as a temporary state (the Spanish and Portuguese verbs *ser* and *estar*)? We are back to the ambivalences that any 'A is B' statement may carry. 'Is' is tricky in English and the ancient Greeks had a field day distinguishing (or failing to) between what we call the identity, the predicative and the existential uses. '2 + 2 *are* 4' is an identity statement (though you have pointed out in some of your papers – Viláça 2018; 2021a – that more may be involved than mere arithmetic). 'Socrates *is* snub-nosed' is predicative. 'Socrates *is*' is a (no longer true) existential statement. And to that analysis others have added others, for instance the locative, that is, statements that inform you of the position of an item (there is a weighty tome by Charles Kahn (1973) about all of this), with some scholars coming away with an overwhelming sense of Greek confusions (not to say of our own), while others hail what they consider to be triumphant clarifications. There is quite a bit too, of course, on differences that already exist within Romance languages on predication, existence and the copula in general.

A: On that kind of difference (between *ser* and *estar*), as far as I know the Wari' do not make it in the same way. They have a verb equivalent to 'exist': *ma'*. Like in the sentence: *Ma' na hwam*, 'There is fish' or 'fish exist'. You say so when, for example, you talk about a fishing spot, or about the outcome of a fishing expedition. I can arrive at someone's house and ask: *Ma' na hwam*? Or, in Wari' style, I may prefer to say through the negative form: *Om na hwam*? (*om* = 'no', 'does not exist'), and they may answer: *Ma' na* ('there is'; 'it exists').

A Wari' will never say something like 'I exist'. When they call me on the phone they might ask: *pe wet ma*? *Pe* is 'to be in some place'; *wet* is 'still'; *ma* is the second-person singular pronoun. The translation could be: 'Are you still there [in Rio]?' That could carry the meaning: 'Oh, you are still alive, although you do not send us any news.' They will never ask me something like: 'are you alive?' It is totally impolite. Although they have a word for it, of course: *e'* means 'to be alive'.

They would say about the jaguar-shaman Orowam, for example: *Kopakao' na Orowam*. *Na* is the third-person singular pronoun. 'Jaguar he Orowam'. People could say about Orowam: '*Kopakao' ina, na Orowam.*' *Ina* is the first-person singular pronoun; *na* is the third-person singular pronoun. The free translation is: 'I am a jaguar, says Orowam.' Usually they prefer the last sentence when the affirmation is something you could have doubts about. So they name the source of it. All their narratives about events in which the narrator did not participate are given in this indirect mode. They could also say about Orowam: '*Jamu pin na Orowam; kopakao' pin na*', which could be translated as: 'Orowam transformed (*jamu*) completely (*pin*). He is completely (*pin*) a jaguar.' We could also express it as 'Orowam jaguarizes' as you mentioned above.

Specifically on transformations, they say, for example: '*Kopakao' paxi na Orowam, kataxik pin na.*' *Kopakao'* is 'jaguar'; *paxi* is 'more or less', 'in the past' or 'not any more'; *na* is the third-person singular pronoun; *kataxik* is a collared peccary (a kind of wild pig); *pin* is 'completely'. The translation could be: 'Orowam used to be a jaguar, but now he is a wild pig.' Orowam, as a shaman, could decide which animal he wants to follow and, as I said, being together with someone (person or animal) involves, as a consequence, the transformation of the body (in the wider sense, which includes not only sharing habits, tastes and food, but also the perspective on the world). If I had asked Orowam about this, he might have said that from his point of view, all species, as humans, look the same to him. That is another interesting point. Usually, when they try to hunt, shamans feel unable to shoot, as all they see are human beings. When they are still training, or in the beginning of their initiation, Wari' shamans could say that they see animals transforming quickly: a tapir turns into a peccary, which turns into a monkey, and so on. Both are different ways to state the same thing: all animals capable of transforming, *jamu*, are equivalent from a shaman's perspective.

P: I suppose quite a few stories suggest that 'shaman' itself is to some extent an open-ended position and there is a spectrum from, as it were, a full-time, dare I say professional, to someone who has the odd shamanic experience.

A: Exactly. As I told you, beginners usually see animals transforming fast, one into another. Considering the point that any transformation relates to a pair (or a multiplicity), not to an individual, the beginner was transforming along with the animals. There were reports of men who were shamans for only a day, just because they related to an animal as if it were a human. Usually that person, afterwards, gets sick and has to be cured by a shaman, who talks with the animals, asking them to leave his relative (the shaman-to-be) alone.

CHAPTER 7

Is Shamanism a Kind of Disease?

P: You talk about the changes in perspectives as understood as changes in bodies, where the shamans circulate fast, but ordinary persons would run the risk of not being able to get back. Was the shaman's unstable vision treated as almost like a disease? How far is his experience mirrored in that of other 'apprentice shamans'? It would surely be too simple to say that those who become shamans were all outsiders or failures.

A: I think I could say yes to both questions. Yes, it is a kind of disease in the beginning. The shaman is in fact someone who got sick (was attacked by an animal double) and was not healed by another shaman (but by the animals themselves). They say that a shaman, by definition, is someone with a strange vision. It usually becomes more stable over the course of a shaman's life. Shamans are not outsiders or failures. They are full members of the society, have families, grow crops, participate in the festivals. They are not, usually, good hunters, for the reason I just told you.

CHAPTER 8

Are There Objects without Perspectives?

P: The question that this then prompts is this. Does the Wari' language mark any differences in the kinds of statements that report different perspectives? On the one hand, some of the problems seem to be problems of translation (from Wari' talk to jaguar talk to tapir talk and so on, and back again). On the other, you have put it that these are not issues of translation so much as of transformation – through the bodies of the beings concerned, as you remark in To'o's case. Is it just the language (or the perspective) that shifts? Or do the objects themselves switch? Or is there no 'object' without a perspective? Which from a Western or modernist point of view would mean there are no objects as such in the first place – for we assume, do we not? – that there can be objects irrespective of perspectives on them.

I might observe that some of the concentration on the disputes about one versus plural worlds does not help. It would be not so much a matter of different ontologies (as in Descola 2013 or in the studies of Viveiros de Castro 1998, 2004, 2014, 2015) as one of the distance between having an ontology and not having one. No objects is not so much an alternative ontology as the rejection of ontologizing in the first place. The problem with modernity (and Greek antiquity, come to that) would be that it presupposes objects in the first place. Which would be a strange conclusion, given that anthropologists have located the problem not in ontology but in epistemology!

A: I would say that for the Wari' there is no object without a perspective. However, this fact is not explicit when you are going about your daily business. People don't think about it when there is no disease or risk or shamanic interventions. So, we could say that sometimes objects are just fixed things, although at other times they have to consider that another being is looking at it differently and then the object becomes just a perspective.

P: Is it possible to say that the original jaguar's body may somehow trump their human vision?

A: As I said, it is not their bodies that change, like, for example, a comic-book superhero, where you can see the body transforming, exploding, changing (including getting a new superhero cloak). It is the kidnapped person who changes their vision and who for specific reasons (like not being well treated by her real relatives) mistakenly sees the jaguar as a person. Let me explain better by talking about an event at which I was present. It happened during my first few months of fieldwork. I and my adopted brother Abrão (To'o and Paletó's son) were talking with the jaguar-shaman Orowam, whom we both called grandfather. I was asking him a lot of questions about the animal-human doubles and Abrão was acting as an interpreter, as at that point I did not have command of the Wari' language. After a few minutes talking, Orowam began to scratch his eyes with both hands. Without knowing the meaning of it, I naively continued to talk. But Abrão reacted immediately, facing Orowam and saying: 'grandfather, this is us, your grandchildren. We are Wari'.' After we left, Abrão explained to me how risky the situation was: Orowam could not see 'right' and was taking us for prey. He was about to jump on us, said Abrão, but fortunately he listened to what Abrão said and reconsidered (taking us as his grandchildren). Neither I nor Abrão saw any change in his body; he was completely our grandfather, as A'ain Tot said about the jaguar-mother who kidnapped her. But Abrão was capable of understanding that his vision (how Orowam saw things and persons) was getting confused, mixed, out of focus, and that this is why he was scratching his eyes. It was as if, like in To'o's mother's case, his different bodies, manifested in different perspectives, were mixed. Better than mixed, we could say that they were alternating fast, like the frames of a film. Abrão once said that the shamans' vision is like images you see on TV.

P: This is helpful, since in this instance the transformations in question do not involve the metamorphosis of the jaguar body from anyone's point of view. Rather, it is Orowam's behaviour that indicates that it is his perspective that has changed.

A: I think both episodes concerning To'o's mum and Orowam suggest that the way you see a body, the shape of the body as an isolated feature, does not tell you everything you need to know about what kind of person you are facing. Behaviour is part of the body, indissociable from the way a person presents themselves to someone else. If you ask Abrão, for example, about what happened to Orowam in front of us, he would say that Orowam was a jaguar. By this, he does not mean that he (Abrão) saw a jaguar body, with spotted fur, but that, knowing previously that Orowam was a jaguar shaman, he understood that the strange way he looked at us meant that he was not seeing us as Wari' persons any more. The obvious conclusion will be that he was not a person himself (from our point of view), but a jaguar.

Let me give you another example. Once I asked Orowam if I could film him talking about his fellow jaguars. I positioned myself in front of him with my camera. As he began to talk, lots of people circled us. Suddenly, he began to look at his left side and talk very low to someone I could not see. I kept my position, but all the Wari' ran to the other side, clearing the area on his left. When I heard the women shouting to their children to run, I realized that his fellow jaguars were there, although I could not see them. The Wari' couldn't either, but they knew what was happening. I kept filming. Orowam began to talk to me, then to the jaguars and then back to me, reporting what the jaguars were saying. One of the things they told him was that he should ask me for compensation for letting me film him. I agreed, of course. Then he told me that he was explaining to the jaguars that I was his granddaughter, a real Wari'. He said so because the jaguars were seeing me as prey and were about to attack me. At this moment, Orowam had his two bodies, or better, his two perspectives, alternating fast, jaguar–human–jaguar–human.

P: Again, that is helpful, in that it shows that the way people behave is key. But that still leaves a problem, because if bodies do not change, how do you explain the event Paletó told you, where the man kidnapped by a tapir succeeded in coming back to his village? He did not just keep acting strangely, eating non-edible food, but as you reported it, his body itself showed signs of the tapir body (his crooked knees)?

A: In that case the double identity manifested itself clearly in a mixed body, though we still have to remember that 'body' covers more than just physical flesh and bones. It is equivalent to the tail To'o's mother saw in her jaguar-nephew. It is a bodily expression of a double perspective, not just from the animal-person, but also from their relatives, who saw the jaguar as an animal. As I said, transformations must be taken in pairs. It is always a complex play of perspectives. The crooked knees are manifestations of his continued strange behaviour.

P: Then again, in their human mode their perceptions would be the same as ours, would they not? At both stages in To'o's story, the jaguar in the jungle and the jaguar transformed, what they see qua human is or should be what *we* see. I take it I have gone wrong at some point.

A: I think that we would better phrase it as humanities instead of humanity. The jaguar *is* human, but of another kind, because it has different habits, which make its body different from Wari' bodies. Although the events could vary widely, the Wari' would say that jaguars always see themselves as humans see themselves. But exactly for this reason it (the jaguar) usually does not see the Wari' as humans, at least not as the same kind of humans as itself, the human-jaguar. That is not only about the physical body, but manners, company, food choices, habits. As I said, the body is a much wider concept for them than for us. So, transformation is a change of habits, of manners. The Wari' define human beings as people with what we call culture, specifically Wari' culture. They all prepare their food, have families, have the same kind of festivals, speak the same language. Like the jaguar that kidnapped To'o's mother and A'ain Tot. It spoke with each of them in Wari' language, it was concerned to feed them, have sex, collect fruits. All of the things that the Wari' do themselves. The difference is that, from the Wari' point of view, jaguars mix things up. They look at blood and call it *chicha*. They are human because they like *chicha* and they are jaguars, meaning another kind of human, because what they see as *chicha* is blood. There were stories about a Wari' who meets an unknown person in the forest, and this person invites them to drink *chicha*. The Wari' accepts with pleasure and everything seems perfectly normal until the *chicha* is offered and the Wari' looks at it and realizes it is in fact blood. Usually the person tries to escape because they realize that the *chicha* giver is a jaguar. Not because they see a tail or fur, but because they know (through myths and narratives) that the kind of human who drinks blood is a jaguar.

P: Where I went astray was in the assumption that the jaguars themselves transformed. The more important transformation is in the vision that certain humans have of whoever they are encountering and how those others are likely to behave. Yet if I go back over your data, there are transformations that are not just a matter of someone's vision changing. So on we go.

A: Don't you think the whole misunderstanding between us is because we still keep considering bodies through the way we think about our own bodies? Fixed entities that could go through changes in form due to sickness, clothing, surgery or ageing, and that this is necessarily something that the person themselves could normally see, and so too could other persons. It is something visible to anyone who is not impaired either objectively or subjectively. It is a 'reality' that exists independently of the relations you go through. Among the Wari' it is more subtle, more relational. Bodies in a way are sometimes capable of sudden changes, not like losing a leg, but like becoming an animal. Don't you think that it is our Western-scientific bias that underlies those questions? What if a body is something else? Do we need to redefine what a body is?

P: I am not so sure that a new definition (of body) is what we need, for at the start of an inquiry that has the effect of putting it into a straitjacket. But it is clear that what counts as a transformation is a key issue, or (I am now inclined to say) a complex of issues. Change of relations is a common factor throughout: but sometimes (perhaps not always) there are physical changes as well as changes in modes of perception.

We cannot tackle 'body' without 'transformation' and 'process' and 'agency', as you have insisted, nor can we do 'health and disease' without 'process' and 'transformation' and 'body'. That introduces considerable complexity and indeed instability into our discussion. But I see that as a positive advantage, as the source of greater insight and deeper revision, one of our principal goals, as I think we agree.

Here it does seem possible and necessary to do justice not just to certain similarities but – as you insist – to very sharp divergences between different conceptions that may be in play. The contrast between an assumption that 'body' must pick out what is stable and the view that bodies are inherently unstable is obviously crucial. We have the Wari' to thank for some important registrations of that instability.

I can chip in with Heraclitus and not just Zhuangzi, but every Chinese writer who recognizes the role of *qi* ('breath' or 'energy') as the ever-changing, undifferentiated origin of any and every differentiation.

Qi is nowadays usually not translated but transliterated, but readers are owed an account of its semantic range. Here is Nathan Sivin in our book *The Way and the Word* (2002: 196) (where he persisted in using the old-fashioned transliteration *ch'i*):

> The untranslatable term *ch'i* was used before 300 BC for a multitude of phenomena: air, breath, smoke, mist, fog, the shades of the dead, cloud forms, more or less everything that is perceptible but intangible; the physical vitalities, whether inborn or derived from food or breath; cosmic forces and climatic influences ... that affect health; and groupings of seasons, flavors, colors, musical modes, and much else. *Ch'i* could be benign and protective, as that proper to the human body was, or pathological, an intangible agent of disease.

To that add: 'Yin-yang and the five phases had, by the end of the first century BC, a consistent, dynamic character as part of the *ch'i* complex. Anything composed of or energized by *ch'i* is yin or yang not absolutely but with reference to some aspect of a pair to which it belonged and in relation to the other member' (ibid., 198–99).

In Chinese cosmogonical stories (as in Chapter 3 of the *Huainanzi*), first of all things are quite undifferentiated. Then they start to differentiate, and that is a matter of the separation of pure, bright, hot *qi* (which becomes heaven) from heavy, turbid, cold *qi* (which becomes earth).

In medical contexts there is talk of a *qi* associated with different parts, or better, functions in the body: heart *qi*, liver *qi*, *qi* of the lungs, spleen, kidneys and so on, as well as the *qi* associated with water, earth and so forth. There is a table of these in Elisabeth Hsu's (2010) *Pulse Diagnosis in Early Chinese Medicine*. Transformations are constantly occurring, so this is an important part of Chinese diagnostics, and therefore also of therapy.

But then the theme of the transformations of animals is further developed in relation to Chinese discussions of good governance, the ideal of sage rulership. There is a great article on this by one of my Cambridge sinologist colleagues, Roel Sterckx, entitled 'Transforming the Beasts: Animals and Music in Early China', in the journal *T'oung Pao* (2000). Sterckx points out how different Chinese discourse on animals is from Aristotle's zoology (though of course, other Greco-Roman discussions of animals share Chinese preoccupations with moral and political issues), and he also collects a good deal of material on Chinese assumptions about transformations in general.

In a piece I contributed to a 2007 special issue of *JRAI* (Lloyd 2007), I had some discussion of how far the Greek concept of *pneuma* resembled or diverged from Chinese *qi*, while pointing out that the Greeks disagreed among themselves. One line of thought considered that the problem was: is *pneuma* an element on a par with earth, water, air or fire? But the Greeks often tended to misrepresent their opponents, particularly the Stoics, who saw the fundamental cosmological principles not as substances so much as interacting processes, the active and passive principles as they called them.

Clearly the multiple resonances of *qi* have implications for Chinese conceptions of the body, but there is the further term *ti*, which can also be used in that connection. That is one of several terms used to talk about the human body (Sivin 1995 and Sommer 2008 discuss these), but it is also used of incorporeal entities, including geometrical figures. In the mathematical classics it is used of the convergence of inscribed regular polygons to the circumference of the circle: the famous problem of whether that convergence is ever complete (I puzzled over this in *Adversaries and Authorities* (Lloyd 1996: 154)). This is a reminder that the range of the agenda of reflection on key issues varies, within limits, between our various target cultures. Your detailed studies of the mathematical abilities of Indigenous populations such as the Wari' address that problem (Vilaça 2021a).

As I have noted before, the standard Greek term for 'body', *sōma*, starts by meaning 'corpse'. It took some time for it to be used more generally for that which is corporeal. Meanwhile, to talk of 'matter' (as opposed to form), the term *hylē* was conscripted, though its original sense was simply 'wood'. The Greeks also used the term *stereon* for 'solid', and that could be applied to three-dimensional but incorporeal items, what we still call (geometrical) solids. (In Plato's *Timaeus* that slide between three-dimensionality to corporeality plays a key role in getting him from the pure geometry of his atomic elements to the constituents of the physical universe.)

A: It seems to me that ideas of flow and unstable pairing are a striking feature of Chinese ontologies, much more than among the Greeks. Am I right? In that sense, Chinese concepts seem to be closer to some Amazonian ones. I remember that Lévi-Strauss (2013), in his collection of essays on Japan, made several parallels between Indigenous Amazonia and the Far East. Some have to do exactly with fluidity.

P: However, he generalized far too much. Neither the Japanese nor the Chinese should be treated as homogeneous entities, let alone ones that can be considered stable over centuries.

CHAPTER 9

Why Are Some Animals Unable to Transform?

P: So let me go back. 'Transformation' for the Wari' seems to involve coming to have another creature's vision, their eyes, if not their body as a whole. Shamans are gifted with the ability to have jaguar's eyes when it is jaguars that they follow, and so analogously with other kinds of animals whom the shamans follow or with whom they eat. But your remarks on the species that do not transform (spider monkeys) suggest that there are limits to the acquisition of other creatures' eyes and bodies. Does that mean that a spider monkey (for instance) always sees its food and drink in a set, stable way, though not necessarily in the way that humans see those items? As you can imagine, the limits of transformations are, for me (with my eyes!), as puzzling as the transformations themselves when they occur.

A: There are animals that are just animals, *karawa*, although they have a heart (*ximixi'*), meaning intelligence, intuition. But they do not have a *jamixi'*, a double, or a capacity to produce a double that has a different appearance from the other body. They never see themselves as humans. They cannot kidnap, they cannot attract the Wari' as if they were people.

P: I would still like to press the question of what makes the difference between those animals that do, and those that do not, have a *jamixi'*.

A: The answer is in myth and in shaman's experiences. That is where they base their knowledge. No shaman in present times has ever seen a spider monkey as a person. As I already said, the spider monkey has its own myth recounting how it lost its humanity. They used to be human, but they kidnapped a Wari' woman and then lost their humanity. All fish are capable of transforming, *jamu*, because they live underwater where the dead live and relate to them as people. Great predators, like the jaguar and the anaconda, are capable of transforming, although they are not edible. Many other transformative or potentially human animals are their preferred prey, as I already told you.

P: You have made it clear that this Wari' view is not a view about animals as a whole, rather about certain ones. That is important as a warning against generalizing about Wari' conceptions of what we consider the animal kingdom. Even so, that raises the further problem of differentiation that I have mentioned.

A: Yes, that is a good point. As I already pointed out, although many animals are always present in shamans' lists of animals with *jamixi'*, meaning they could act as humans, some other ones are included on certain occasions, depending on some particular shaman's experience. It is not a closed set. Differently from what you say about the Greeks, in Amazonia transformations are in the present (not posthumous, although they may happen posthumously) and reversible. And to be recognized as such, a transformation has to include a third point of view.

P: The idea about the reversibility of transformations in the present is clearly crucial. In many cases of Greco-Roman transformations, they are permanent. Daphne as a girl fleeing the lecherous Apollo becomes a laurel tree (and stays as such). But in the Pythagorean transmigration of souls an individual may on death become one type of creature, but after another life be reborn as a different one – struggling to get back up the hierarchy of more noble animals and hopefully eventually escaping the bitter cycle of rebirth altogether. Now there's a different message for us!

A: That is an important point. It should be stressed, however, that some Amazonian peoples have the idea that a dead person becomes an animal, and then another one, and then another until they disappear.

CHAPTER 10

Do Transformations Need Proof? Are Shamans and Healers Ever Doubted?

P: Earlier, in the chapter I quoted before, Zhuangzi had cast doubt on whether any assertions or denials can be made, even though he had also said that we have somehow to 'rely on' things ('depend on them' in the words of the penultimate para.). Throughout, what the text gives with one hand it takes away with the other. In view of this, one might insist that insisting on a determinate interpretation is barking up the wrong tree.

A: 'How to rely on things' is also a very Amerindian problem. For the Wari' the answer will be making kin and allies, as much as you can. This is the way to constitute a stable group of people who have a shared perspective and can rely on each other (with exceptions, of course, as animals could fake kinship in order to carry out a kidnapping). Stability depends not on creating rules and laws (and classifications) but on acting towards making similar bodies, which, in the extended sense, as I said, includes behaviour. For that reason, marrying, having many kids, making others into in-laws (not always so reliable, we know) is so important. Not just for material survival, as in cooperation, but for creating more or less, or at least temporarily, stable perspectives. Their 'psychoanalysis' is necessarily collective and is based on the body (the extended body).

P: There is still a strong sense that in certain contexts the Wari' cannot be sure who or what they are dealing with – and that appears to be not only in cases where shamans following their doubles are concerned. But that prompts me to ask the more general question. How far is it the case that it is just unacceptably rude to challenge what someone has said, the stories that they tell? Shamans are sometimes doubted, are they not? But within what limits are they confronted by denial? I ask in part because of a similarity and a difference with an ancient Greek instance. Let me explain.

In Greece too, as is also known for Amazonian shamanism, there are cases where healers suck material from the sick person's body to purify them, rid them of the peccant stuff that is causing the illness. But then in one such report in the Hippocratic Corpus the author adds the comment 'deception'. In the medical marketplace that developed in the ancient Greek world (which is often very conscious of non-Greek ideas and practices on their doorstep) competitiveness is more or less obligatory. This is not just to do with literacy – the exchanges and the rivalries are mostly mediated in the oral mode. Nor would I say that the rivalries are purely the product of being exposed to other cultures. But in the Greek case we have to remember that political leaders in many city states had to give an account (financial and otherwise) of their behaviour at the end of their tenure of office, and it would be hard to deny that the custom of such challenges had an impact in other areas of life. That custom could hardly develop in a group numbering in the hundreds rather than the tens of thousands, so scale is clearly important. But surely that is not the only factor at work.

It is on the cards, for the Wari' themselves, isn't it, to say that some stories that imply exotic experiences, whether of shamans or of transforming animals, are just fabrications cooked up by individuals anxious to claim superior knowledge for themselves and to use their positions to manipulate and control their fellow humans. It is not just appearances that deceive, but also humans. But although we may all be subject to gullibility some of the time, I don't suppose any group anywhere could survive if everyone was gullible all the time. The ethnographic reports are full of accounts that show just how alert people are to the possibility of lies and deception, of fake shamans talking about fake jaguars.

A: Rivalries and disputes on diagnosis do exist among the Wari' and other Amazonian people. But they almost never take the form of direct confrontation. Lévi-Strauss's piece on the shaman Quesalid and his magic seems to me something inconceivable for the Wari'. Quesalid started out doubting the powers of the shamans of neighbouring tribes, but then he learned to do the same as them – perform their tricks as he originally thought – and he discovered he could do so successfully.

Doubts exist, of course, but as far as I observed, they are always, in the case of shamans, the outcome of the consequences or results of a cure. One shaman says something about the cause of the disease, another one says something else. There is no talk about one being right and the other wrong. Shamans do not deceive because there are always many possibilities. Visions depend on which animal the shaman is following, meaning that he is eating and living among them. They are seeing different things (together with their companion animals, who are helping each shaman with the cures). The key question is: after which session does the sick person feel better? This is what indicates who is more effective (or has the best companions). It was not a matter of being right or wrong. And furthermore: usually the shamans cure in pairs. Shamans are careful making their diagnosis. They ask what the sick persons have eaten, killed or done in the past few days. Even so, if a cure does not succeed, they can always attribute it to some new event they had not considered before. In sum, I would say that it is rude to contest a shaman's vision, but not because you are accusing him of being a liar, but because nobody knows exactly what is going on. Many visions and perspectives are in play: each shaman's animal double, the internal moral relationships between humans, the relation between humans and animals. Some cases involve the aggression of more than one species. During healing rituals, the shamans speak out loud all the time, sometimes to their animal companions, at other times to the audience, giving them moral lectures (why did you have extra-conjugal sex?). It is a mixture of voices and the audience seems not to pay attention. There are not formal speeches among them. The shamans address no one in particular. I saw people dancing to Brazilian music during a healing session: the sick person was in the middle of the place, lying down, surrounded by shamans, and people were dancing Brazilian *forró* around them. The shamans do not see it as disrespect, although I was always in shock.

Nowadays (I am referring to the time after 2001), being Christians, the Christianized Wari' say that in the old days people were deceived by the devil. What shamans saw was not real, it was the devil who acted upon them to make them see false images. They would never think of a shaman deceiving people before. It was about being or not being effective, not about being false.

P: Let me insist on the basis for authority a bit more. Aren't there any circumstances where the question of who is right arises? We should not say that this never arises for the Wari', should we? The fact that challenges to veracity and correctness are routine and institutionalized in many contexts in ancient Greek society is a feature of how they organize social relations. But this is a matter of degree, it seems to me.

A: When my older son, Francisco, was 1 year old, he had a urinary infection. My grandfather shaman-jaguar, Orowam, examined him and said that he had played on what he saw as mud, but in fact he was on top of some animal's (I think an armadillo's) territory or house. However, his treatment did not cure him.

P: When people saw he was not cured, wasn't there a question of trust at stake?

A: From my point of view, yes, there was a question of truth, as I decided to treat my son with antibiotics. But when Francisco's symptoms remained after the shamanic cure, no one said that they did not trust Orowam or that he was deceiving us. They would say: who knows what else that kid was stepping on? So it is a matter of a lack of complete information: it was not the shaman's fault. Truth is a relational matter. In that case, could we talk about 'truth', the way we understand it, as something incontestable?

P: The sociological questions are sometimes investigable – at least I think I can get some way in plotting the circumstances of proving and doubting of different kinds in ancient Greece and China, and come to that Babylonia, Egypt, India – in each case, the answers are different: isn't that refreshing! And I am sure you can do the same for the Wari' and make points about the differences to be found in different Amazonian communities – let alone further afield. As far as the Wari' themselves are concerned, you say they are not confrontational. But how does authority get to be established and maintained?

A: Authority is dispersed and depends on experience, especially such matters as the capacity to provide for a family, narrative skills, good relations. A reliable person is someone who has plenty of relations and does not quarrel and fight (inside the village or within the close social group), not necessarily a shaman. Warriors, meaning people who had already killed an enemy, were particularly prestigious and usually had several wives, as the bride's father trusted that such a man would be a good provider. There is no canon, no repertoire of male songs, no sages. Everyone could be right or wrong, or even partially right or wrong. But they do not say this to someone to their face. They do gossip. There is no confrontation, unless someone becomes ill. Then, facing death, they could say that a certain person did witchcraft. Usually a variety of reasons are invoked for accusations of sorcery. The person who is possibly a sorcerer is a loner, stingy, and so on. Consequently, what he says is usually not true. But that is not because of the content of his sayings but because of his relational world.

As I already said, the Wari' have a word for true: *iri'*. But they have a word for lying too: *mixein*. They also have a word that could be translated by 'to believe': *howa*. It is more to believe in a person than in what is being said. That person is a good person, I follow them. The missionaries use it in the sense of believing in God. Of course, the missionaries' agenda is quite different from mine. They are out to convert, while my aim is understanding, for which respect for the Wari''s views is essential. The assumption of those who are out to convert is that they are right and others are wrong. The anthropologist makes no such assumption: nor should the philosopher.

Talking about lies, the word *mixein* can sometimes be replaced by *waraju*, 'to play'. *Mixein* has the same fluid meaning. A person can tell a joke or make up a story for fun and the others will say, laughing: *mixein ma* ('you are lying'), or even *waraju ma* ('you are kidding!'). When they are angry they can be more serious about those terms, accusing someone of being a liar, for example. Now, in Christian times, both words have acquired a very rigid meaning, of course. The devil *mixein*. God always tells the truth: *Iri' o* (true) *na ka tomi* (says) *Iri' Jam* (God). The name for God, made by the missionaries but approved by the Wari', has the *Iri'* in it. What I understood talking to the missionaries themselves is that their intention with the translation was to name God as 'the true spirit', but that was not exactly what the term conveyed. In fact, the precise translation of *Iri'*

Jam made by the Wari' was 'the true invisible'; *jam* meaning invisible, 'ex-body'.

If we get to the missionaries, then proof has a place. They write in their books about proof: how can we know that God was so powerful and created everything? By the outcomes of his creation, they say: animals, forests, people. The Wari' used to say: before we thought that things existed for no reason, that animals were always there, trees too. Now, becoming Christians, they know that the ancestors did not know things, because they did not know that it was God who created everything. This is what a 33-year-old man said to me:

> The ancient ones [*hwanana*] did not know properly. It was the devil [*kaxikon jam*] who hampered them so they would not hear the speech [*kapijakon*] of *Iri' Jam*. They believed [*howa*] in Pinom [a mythic figure]. Where is Pinom? He's never seen. But the earth that God created, the water, the fish, all of that can be seen. That's why it is true [*iri' o*]. That of *hwanana* is only a story, it's not true.

P: Your point that shamans often heal together, in pairs, is suggestive: in ancient Greece a claim to being a Master of Truth often meant excluding everyone else. Your final remark about the contexts in which conversations of this type crop up does suggest to me that that point is worth taking further. We surely have to bear in mind that matter-of-fact discourse is just one type of discourse and that when people seriously grapple with how to make sense of experience they can move into a different register. Don't we all? Different rules of politeness apply. Quarrelling about what happens to the dead, yours and other peoples', or about the gods, does not put food on the table.

A: You are right, although I think that even considering the contexts, the Wari' world functions in a manner that is very different from ours (yours and mine). Even now, being Christians and 'kind of modern', they continue to surprise me with some reports. Last time we met, my brother Abrão said that he was with someone who saw fish transforming into arms and hands in the water (where the dead used to live).

P: But was Abrão's interlocutor a shaman? Seems likely. You pick up the point about not quarrelling, but (a) there are disagreements that you frequently document, and (b) you pointed out to me that the Wari' idea of flourishing includes aggressive, even warlike behaviour: I understood you to imply that perfect peace would be boring.

A: Regarding Abrão's companion, he was not a shaman, but his friend. That is why Abrão was so impressed. He did not say that his friend was turning into a shaman, as Abrão is now a Christian. But he could have said that in the past. Regarding the other point, saying that they quarrel does not mean that they do not trust people's vision. They often quarrel about domestic stuff, like sexual acts outside marriage, being stingy, accusing people of hiding food and so on. Not about who saw what. War is not considered a kind of quarrel. Enemies are not considered human beings of the same type as the Wari', but of the animal's kind. Enemies, *wijam*, are part of the category of *karawa*, animals, prey, food. Making war is like going to hunt. People have, towards the enemies, an intrinsic or given animosity. When I say that life without conflicts is boring for them, I don't mean internal ones, fights between themselves, but conflicts directed to the outside, either with 'foreigners', which is how they call the Wari' from different geographical groups, or with enemies, whites and Indians in general.

P: You question whether if truth belongs to the person or to a set of relations, we can still talk of it as truth. But in English and modern European vernaculars, as well as in ancient Greece and China, terms that are used to talk of 'true' statements (as opposed to false ones) are also used in the context of remarks for instance about 'true' friends, genuine ones you can rely on. There is usually a deep concern with distinguishing true friendship or virtue or sagehood from what merely seems to be that, and this applies not just to moral qualities. How do we distinguish true diamonds, true jade, true gold, from fakes? It is really only certain philosophers, starting with some Greeks, who wanted to stipulate that truth is a property of propositions alone, and why they sought to do so is a long story wherein their claims to superior knowledge figure prominently, including, as you have guessed, their command of a style of 'proof' that aimed at incontrovertibility! Of course the methods of verification differ. Saying who ranks as a true friend is not a matter of logic. You judge your friends by their behaviour, and true friends may well need on occasion to tell fibs. In what you have told me about Wari' *iri'*, I see no signs of confusion or muddle. But it is interesting that they don't make a great fuss about this in some contexts where some ancient Greeks would.

A: Right. But don't we differentiate the status of truth, like in science, from truth, like in a true friend? We are conscious that the first one is an absolute (or more or less so) truth, that should apply to anyone, and the second is a relative one. What if we don't have that differentiation, as among the Wari'?

It is normal for a person to lie, when, for example, someone asks for food and the person says they have no food, although the one who is asking knows that they do. But this is far better than to deny feeding the person, as you will then be accused of avarice. You cannot lie several times anyway, or you will be accused of being stingy.

I was in a virtual debate today regarding the Yanomami (with a student and colleagues) and we were talking about this. They concluded that for the Yanomami, any statement that is empirically false is defined by the term 'lie', although there is no moral judgement. One of my colleagues, who knew the Yanomami well, said that they once asked him when an expected plane was coming and he gave the information that it was to be tomorrow. The plane did not come due to the weather, and they called him a liar, although conscious that it had not come due to the weather. They do not have the moral view that it is good to say the truth and bad to lie. The term for 'lie' covers more than ours, as it includes 'deceive'. A different theory of mind. One of my colleagues reminded us of the book by Ellen Basso (1987), *In Favor of Deceit*, about the trickster in Kalapalo mythology (the Kalapalo are a Xingu Indigenous people in central Brazil).

P: There are several important points. Let me pick out two. (1) We must be careful not to take it that *all* 'science' achieves 'absolute truth'. Science is not a single unified block of true, well-formed statements, though many Westerners like to portray it as such, forgetting that much of what – correctly – passes as science is provisional, probabilistic, liable to be revised. (2) 'Lie' in English implies an *intention* to deceive. 'Untruth' is a wider term encompassing lies but also falsehoods where there is no such intention – as would be the case with your colleague. It looks as if 'lie' is a misleading translation of what he was accused of, for as you say the Yanomami do not associate lying with immorality.

A: That is a good point: it might be a bad translation. But people who know the language did think it was the best one. In Portuguese, it could be: *ele se enganou* ('he was mistaken'), which means he had no intention to lie, that the person was confused, either by his own mind or by an outsider.

P: Maybe the term 'deceive' is ambiguous too here. Recall that when the French say *j'étais deçu* we would often translate it as 'I was disappointed' – when I have not actively been led astray by someone conveying untruths.

A: In Portuguese the word for 'deceive' would be *desapontado*, which means that you were expecting something and received another thing, one you do not want or like. An example would be when you think a person is brilliant and you discover they are stupid or bad.

P: Ancient Greeks were convinced that truth-telling was a cardinal virtue for the Persians. The Greeks themselves had this notion of *metis* or 'cunning intelligence' for an ability they generally admired – winning, including by cheating, provided you were not found out. Throughout the *Odyssey* Odysseus is liable to lie through his teeth, including to Athena, though she is not taken in. So quite what moral valence will be attached by any given group to lies and truth in any context is an open question, to which the answer varies.

A: That is a very important point: lying as a capacity. Isn't it what fiction writers do? As far as I know, the Wari' do not praise that capacity. When two people recount a story differently, they attribute it to different experiences, points of view. I realize more and more that all their experiences are based on the presupposition of an unstable world, made of different experiences that do not sum up, but stay side by side.

P: I am impressed too with F. Barth (1975) on the Baktaman on this problem. Lies are part and parcel of the complex processes of initiation. Baktaman individuals go through not just one or two rites of initiation but a whole series of them. At each stage they are informed of certain rules and truths, but it sometimes happens that at the next stage they are told that what they have learned was false, even that it has involved the breaking of a strict taboo. This means one can never know if one has got to the bottom of it and reached a stable set of items of knowledge and ways of behaving by which to live a good life.

How far do the Wari' engage in play-talk with young children? In some societies the fact that talking with children is play-talk gives play-talk in other contexts a bad reputation: but that is not necessarily the case. How children are treated is generally a very good way into an inquiry into the (adult) values in any given group.

A: I don't know much about the Wari' playing with children. But I know that they lie to them, saying for example that the enemy (whites in general) will take them away if they do not behave. The child cries and the adult laughs. They don't see it as bad.

P: I had a rather different question in mind, which was the extent to which the Wari' tell stories to the kids that no one takes as literal fact, but everyone enjoys as good fun (with some possible serious messages thrown in).

A: The stories they used to tell them are either myths or real events. In terms of talk, they take children as adults. Children can listen to any conversation, and see births, deaths and fights.

CHAPTER 11

Are Transformations Analogous to Miracles? Is It All about Believing?

P: Consider again To'o's mother making blood into *chicha*. Would it be absurd to compare this to such examples as some of the miracle cures described in pagan and Christian sources? Of course the immense difference is that they were often propaganda, and there is no trace of that (is there?) with To'o's mum.

A: I suppose people doing a miracle are conscious of what they are doing and focus on the matter itself. Like an exhibition, as you say. But for To'o's mother, it did not work this way. She was just drinking her *chicha*. It was her daughter who saw the transformation.

P: Take the case of transubstantiation, for example. The communicant's body does not change: the wine does, but the shaman's 'body' does transform according to the Wari'. Again, what if we consider that these transformations do not concern bodies in the first place, but merely the behaviour and beliefs of the agents concerned? Would that be a possible interpretation? Perhaps not. But modern Nobel-prizewinning physicists or even some anthropologists, if they are good Catholics, accept transubstantiation. The non-believer sees the wine as wine, the believer sees it as the blood of Christ. Actually, different Christian sects have quite different stories to tell about how exactly to interpret the 'miracle' involved, although for all Catholics transubstantiation implies that one has occurred, one that is re-enacted every time the Mass is celebrated. That serves as a forceful reminder that there are limits to the domains over which the discourse of science rules even today.

A: I guess that in the case of Catholic scientists, they experience it as two different aspects of their lives that do not impinge on one another. Or if they do get to be mixed up they relate somehow to different levels. In that case spiritual life is cordoned off from science, so we are free to believe whatever we like provided that it does not concern matter, 'reality', bodies. Among the Wari', we can talk not just about individual perspectives, but of different worlds: the human's world and the jaguar's world are different and, except for shamans, the Wari' strive to keep them apart. They strive exactly because they know that they are not apart at all, as they could interpenetrate one another suddenly.

P: Compartmentalizing (the spiritual world versus the scientific one) has to face down the philosophical difficulty that this looks like allowing sheer inconsistency or self-contradiction. Like the demand for strict definition, this is a two-edged sword. For sometimes we do want to recognize different levels of discourse (the registers I was going on about). I want to keep a continuity between discourses as far as possible, while accepting that degrees and modes of verifiability differ.

A: We should keep them in continuity, but do people who live in different worlds (like science and religion) think they are in continuity? I don't know.

P: Of course some do and some don't. There are plenty of scientists who work quite hard on the theme that science and religion are complementary to one another, though time was when many, perhaps even most scientists saw them as incompatible, irreconcilable. But if we think of the key contrast as one between science and *philosophy*, there may be less of a temptation to be hung up on contrast and competitiveness, even though some go for that even there.

You say that the Wari' who became Christians say that they 'trust' in God. Why do the Wari' believe in what the missionaries told them? Presumably they do not always do so. But how come the missionaries are not dismissed as just animals, *karawa*, as the Wari' used to see the whites in general? The Wari' believe that God talk is *iri'*, true, because you can see the things God created, animals, plants, humans and so on. But they presumably do not believe, or are not told, that the missionaries themselves created things? Is their prestige a matter of their superior (?) knowledge of technology, medicines, the modern world? I recall that in the Wari' conversion to Christianity, healing prevalent diseases played an important part, just as it also did in the opposite direction in their reverting to their original beliefs after their first conversion. Or have I misremembered?

A: In the beginning, all that the missionaries had to convince the Wari' was antibiotics and technology. They gave medicines to nearly dead persons and they were cured a couple of days afterwards. And they say: it was God who cured you. It all happened not during normal times, but during a time when the Wari' were losing lots of people, who either had been shot or were ill. Their world was changing and they wanted to try new sources of power.

CHAPTER 12

Is Proof Linked to Literacy?

P: 'Proof' is absolutely crucial to our inquiry. I have gone on at length about how in certain areas of Greek philosophy, maths and science, absolutely knock-down, 'incontrovertible' (*anexelenktos*) demonstration, depending on self-evident premises and valid deduction, was the gold standard. What was merely persuasive was not good enough (Plato in the forefront: what an extraordinary idea that was!), at least for those who advocated that standard and who generally thought it was within their reach (a certain style of mathematics was the model). But from many points of view that goal of incontrovertible demonstration was just crazy. Of course it was not that difficult, once you got the hang of it, to distinguish between valid and invalid deductions or inferences. But self-evident premises? Such as 'take equals from equals and equals remain' (a stock example). Where were they to be found in fields such as theology (wow), medicine and indeed elsewhere in science?

What you need in practice (as orators and politicians in ancient Greece show they appreciated) was something very different: 'proof', as we say, 'beyond reasonable doubt' – to establish what happened, or guilt or innocence, which has nothing to do with self-evident axioms. Which of course takes us to … doubt. That doubt may be about the evidence for a remark or the trustworthiness of the person making it (cf. Williams 2002 on 'truthfulness') or may concern some deeper sense of just how far human understanding reaches. When, in any given group or society, is it possible to doubt what someone has asserted, or how they have represented how we should behave? When, conversely, is it totally impolite to do so, or ruled out as insulting, insufferable? When, on the contrary, is it permitted, even encouraged, and if so, permitted to whom and in what contexts (cf. court jesters), and especially within what limits? (It is standard practice in many classical Chinese texts to criticize others by suggesting that while they have grasped some of the truth, they have not grasped the whole.)

In the bad old early days of anthropology, 'primitives' were regularly accused of superstition, gullibility, an incapacity to step back and review what was traditionally accepted: the polite-sounding way of downgrading them was via the notion of a different mentality, though that was not really polite at all since it still often carried the label 'primitive'. So when Evans-Pritchard (1937) identified widespread scepticism at least about individual witches among the Azande, that substantially undermined some earlier sweeping generalizations, though to be sure, EP did also talk of a lack of scepticism about witchcraft as a whole. Ditto Lévi-Strauss on Quesalid as we mentioned before.

But this directs attention to a raft of questions: are there in any given group particular individuals or groups who have somehow attained unchallengeable status? And if so, how did they do that? (By birth or apprenticeship or revelation or sheer bluff?) What about the relevance of the scale of the society in question (for scale seems a necessary condition for pluralism: or is it? Does it depend on the nature of the pluralism in question?) Does the availability of transcription, written records, make a difference (Goody 1977) in that it allows a different style of checking about (a) what was actually asserted or claimed and (b) what has passed as the truth or the correct answers to questions of how to behave? (But we should remember that written texts, when treated as canonical or authoritative, may well block criticism and scepticism.)

A: As I already told you, among the Wari' reliable persons are those who are good providers, who support their relatives, who are good hunters or better, warriors. It is not something given by birth and there is no class of sages. Passing on to Goody's arguments in *The Domestication of the Savage Mind* on the effects of literacy, they are controversial as we know. One of them is that illiterate people do not make final and closed conclusions because they cannot have to hand all the different arguments that have been given orally. They cannot synthesize them, for they do not have them written down on paper, which serves as an aide-memoire. Even considering the heavy and sometimes well-aimed criticisms of his theory, I think he had a point, although I am not sure the anti-synthesis ethos he correctly grasped is due solely to non-literacy. See, for example, Wari' maths, which I have explored in several works. Even now that they can write, when they count in their language, quantities become imprecise and indeterminate. When the language remains, it is not so easy to change just because you have become literate.

P: Of course, this is important and there is much that can and should be said about the oral background to classical Greek and Chinese literary texts. But you will have registered that while you find the differences between oral and literate relevant, I have found myself more impressed than I originally expected at the continuities. A spectrum, for me, not a complete radical break.

A: You are right, and we have lots of good criticism of Goody's strong claims. To begin with, knowing how to read and write does not mean that a person is literate. I don't think that the Wari' as a whole are literate, although many young people can read and write. They do not care for written things (the Bible is an exception since it is more than that, it is the word of God on paper, and they certainly care about that). They don't care about reading books, they do not like to write. Literacy is not part of their daily lives, only when they are at school or the university. Literate people have literacy as a central part of their lives. It is different, isn't it?

P: Certainly, although there are lots of people who live in societies where it is normal to be able to read and write, but who hardly use those skills in daily life at all. That must be true of thousands of smallholders and subsistence farmers in rural areas of even 'developed' European countries. The next question your final remark prompts is, then, what difference does literacy make? Do we answer that at the level of social interactions? Or of cognitive structures? I don't see the contents of beliefs or theories being changed by literacy: rather the ways in which they are manipulated, referred to, used.

A: I partially agree. Myths are always transforming, depending on the narrator, the audience, the context. Literacy does not change those oral narratives. But now young people sometimes write down myths for school tasks, and they can easily compare the versions and discuss the differences if they feel like doing so. Sometimes the Wari' teachers use some narratives from my books. Then they come up with questions to be answered by the students. The questions are very school-minded and not Wari'-minded, if I can express myself like that. Like: who stole the fruit? What did X do to his brother? The way of dealing with the narrative changes, although the narrative remains the same. The relevant questions also shift. Those questions are completely different from the ones I heard in the past when the myths were orally recounted by grandfathers and fathers to children. The questions were usually: didn't he see that the person was a jaguar? How could he climb that tree?

P: Contexts may be crucial. Lying in a court of law – or in a king's court (when there are such things) – carries a different valence from fibbing about what you were doing in the forest or hiding the food you had just denied having.

A: Let's take Bateson's (1972) 'Metalogues', which have worked as an implicit inspiration for our own dialogue. In all of them he is talking to his child daughter and they ask each other apparently naive questions that in fact are deep philosophical questions. In one of them they talk about the reality or not of a ballerina becoming a swan when dancing. At that point he draws on the language of sacraments. That is a reminder that we have to bear in mind the register and the context in which all these questions get to be discussed among my friends, the Wari'.

However, I would not say that the Wari' have that kind of conversation about transformations in a kind of sacred or ritual setting, like the ballet theatre. They (used to) talk about it in their daily conversations, if something prompted the subject (like if someone went out hunting and did not come home for some time). Or talking with me, or when commenting on a myth (saying: I saw it myself; meaning, so-and-so animal transforming in the present). They do not believe (or disbelieve) in what is being said. They just listen, ask questions, laugh and then repeat the story if the occasion arises. Someone listening (like the Christians today) could just be interested and say that the elders were strange (*xirak*), or that it was the devil, or that the person is lying. Whatever. And no one is going to fight to prove anything. No discussions, just an exchange of experiences and then silence. No regrets regarding doubting.

CHAPTER 13

Could These Transformations Be Compared to Those in Literary Fiction?

A: We can also ask what the status of transformations is as they appear in fictional literature or poetry. An example would be Kafka's story of the metamorphosis into a cockroach (1935). Did people really think that Zhuangzi became a butterfly or has a butterfly double? Does that have the same reality for listeners or readers as the Wari' becoming a jaguar? What kind of transformation are we talking about? Isn't it better to differentiate them in order not to lose sight of their peculiarities?

P: On transformations in literature from Zhuangzi to Kafka, I agree that there are tons of them, with very different resonances to be sure. So readers will bring a whole different load of baggage to their understandings. I agree too that once a transformation is recorded, that makes a difference, and certainly the ways that authors play with them differ. The theme of disgust that is so strong in the Kafka (is it not?) is absent from Zhuangzi. Where Zhuangzi is concerned the story undermines his Zhuangzi-hood (I mean the idea that he is a stable entity) as well as the butterfly-hood of butterflies (who are after all transient and transformative creatures). There is far more to this than I am mentioning here.

A: It is one thing to read Kafka and think about transformations and instability. It is quite another to be in the forest and to be afraid of being kidnapped by a jaguar who passes as your mother. This is radically different, I think.

P: True, true. But there are the forests of our minds, and not just Kafka's own mind.

A: Right, but the Wari' do not have forests of the mind. Just bodies, everywhere. I think it all depends on how we see these things affecting the present world or people's daily lives. We could say that in this biomedical world we live in, we consider fiction something invented and for that reason incapable of affecting the real world (again, for a typical well-educated urban person). For the Wari', myth is true, it is there, it comes back, it moves. Until the arrival of Christianity, there was no doubt about it. The proof is disease, dream, death.

P: As Bernard Williams (2002) argued in *Truth and Truthfulness*, 'truth' may look a simple concept but is anything but (it carries all sorts of implications about 'reality', 'objectivity', even our old non-friend 'ontology'). His argument was to shift the focus rather on truthfulness, sincerity, the avoidance of deception. One question the ethnography raises is at what point the discourse used in the telling and enacting of the myth is recognized to be, as we have put it before, in a different register. It can be recognized as deeply serious but also appreciated to be somehow different from mundane talk, can it not?

A: We could say that it all depends on the register of the discourse. Among the Wari', what differentiates myth narratives from historical and present ones is that people do not claim to personally know (or to know someone who has known) the characters. They say it is a story from a long time ago. It is not less real than the present ones, but it lacks a way of proving it (relations). The proof comes from present events that attest to the continuity of the myth, or the veracity of the relations or powers present in the myth.

P: But are all the lessons we might pick up from our travels just matters of what we call the imagination? Maybe some will conclude just that. Yet a further moral we can derive from our explorations is the questionability of the sharpest divide between imagination and reality, or to locate the issue in more academic terms, between science and philosophy, science and morality, science and poetry (even). Values are implicit if not explicit in every area of human experience. Of course we do not deduce value judgements directly from the study of distant galaxies or of microbes. But insofar as we can learn from our explorations we are enlarging our understanding of who we are ourselves, not in some grand scheme of things (for there is no such scheme) but rather in relation to our environment, our neighbours, to those who consider themselves our 'enemies' as well as our friends.

CHAPTER 14

Should We Talk about Ontologies When Faced with a World in Flux?

P: On epistemology and ontology the philosophers would insist that the question of the bases of knowledge-claims about what is can and should be distinguished from the question of what there is itself. The first leads into a discussion of perception, reasoning, authority and the like, which is independent of the position adopted on the objects of knowledge, though related to be sure.

When the Wari' say that 'Orowam jaguarizes completely' (a possible translation of *kopakao'* (jaguar) *pin* (completely) *na* (he) *Orowam*, as you've suggested), that shows that it is not just a matter of calling, but of being, or perhaps more accurately, of becoming. No wonder the Wari' have an expression to confirm that the transformation is complete, namely *pin* (as well as the term *jamu*, which means 'to transform'). With *pin* in play, that seems to mean that he has completed the jaguarizing, when that means turning into a jaguar. If so, that gives (to me at least) a very strong confirmation that the Wari' live in a world of transforming beings. That would have consequences for how things are called, but more importantly and directly, consequences for how they are and how they become. So on this reading, the language prompts and facilitates (but it would be wrong to say necessitates) an ontology of becoming.

A: I think you are right.

P: Of course ancient Greeks too can go on about becoming (the verb is *gignesthai*; the noun, of course, *genesis*), and Heraclitus and later the Stoics did see process and flux everywhere. But most of the heavyweight philosophers drew a strong contrast between becoming and being, privileging the latter, often with the argument that if things are in flux, then they cannot be known. That is the key idea that had such momentous consequences for later Western thought.

A: I might say that the Wari', from their point of view, would not say that some things or all things are in flux. Corn is always corn; *chicha* is *chicha*, blood is blood, for someone in a specific situation. But if they change the position, the thing changes too. When I say that everyone knows that blood is *chicha* for the jaguar, it is because they hear the shamans saying that and they trust their vision. The shamans are the ones who can quickly alternate the perspectives. It is not just that they have both, but they can circulate among them, know the difference of perspectives and then translate it to the Wari'. In that sense they are beings of becoming, but only because they do it every day with low risk. Everyone else could experience the change of perspectives, but with a high risk of a definitive passage to the other side, which usually means death and the end of their existence among their original relatives (and the making of kin among the animals).

As I've already noted, an apprentice shaman usually has a very unstable vision. I have a narrative from a shaman (the son of my other father, Wan e', Paletó's elder brother) who at the time was sitting behind his wife, who was telling me that her husband was not a good hunter. In his defence he said that he would look at an animal and see a paca and prepare to shoot, but then it would not be a paca any more, but a white-lipped peccary; then a tapir. He did not mean that the animal would transform from one thing to another, but that his vision was unstable. His transforming list also included a man as a possible target, and at that point he gave up. It is not exactly the world that is changing, but an event that happens between the shaman and the animals. As I said, transformations occur in pairs or multiplicities. Do you think we can phrase it in terms of a world of becoming, not of being? Are these unstable ontologies or unstable persons?

P: I note that the comments thus far in this section are not so much about perspectivism as about becoming (versus presumed stable being). So an extra move is required to get to the points that are especially relevant to perspectives. Everyone knows that for the jaguar, blood is *chicha*. It is striking that while you highlight lots of occasions when the Wari' distinguish between what they have directly and personally experienced and what has just been reported to them, those occasions do not seem to include those in which the jaguar drinking *chicha* is involved. They see jaguars drinking blood, but they know that for the jaguar this is *chicha*. Shamans may jaguarize and jaguars shamanize: does that allow one to say that blood may *chicha*-ize? In which case *chicha* should blood-ize. Except that blood and *chicha* are perceived rather than perceivers.

A: Yes, the Wari' could say: *tokwa na wik*; *tokwa* is *chicha* and *wik* is blood, so this literally means '*chicha* is blood'. What they are saying is that the blood becomes *chicha* for the jaguar. Let's go back to the To'o's mother event, when she drank blood and spat *chicha* remains. She kind of transformed one thing into another inside her body and spat not *chicha* itself, but what remains when we make or drink *chicha*. I first listened to this story in the house where I lived with Paletó and To'o in Sagarana village. She was excited to tell me it. Then she repeated it in front of many people when we were at the house of A'ain Tot, who had experienced a jaguar-mother. As I said, they like the little funny details. It is in situations like this that children, for example, learn that blood is *chicha* for the jaguar. From my point of view To'o's mother became a kind of living body dictionary, revealing not the instability of things, but the duplicity of her body or vision. Or better, what was happening involved not just herself, but also the objects (blood and *chicha*) and the observer, her daughter. There is a set of perspectives in play and transformation involves all of them, not just the mother or the objects taken separately.

P: You remark pertinently that it is not the world that changes, but the person and their positions, and end by asking whether it is a matter of unstable ontologies or unstable persons. To which I would comment first that surely in the ontological explorations of Eduardo Viveiros de Castro and others (you included), the claim is that the world the Wari' and others live in is different (from ours). That might suggest that their ontology *is* stable, although (1) that encompasses different worlds for humans and animals and (2) people – and some animals at least – seem to go in and out of 'it/theirs'. Their bodies are subject to transformation – at least that is true of those of jaguars when they go in for abduction.

A: Thank you for this. I never know how to put it. I would say that they have a stable ontology that at the same time is multiple, meaning that this ontology of theirs (the people born Wari') includes the knowledge that other beings live in a different material world (could we say that?), or have different perceptions of what for them is the world. I really think that point is worth exploring further.

P: Then when we get to To'o's mother, she seems to do the transformations in her own body, where (again) you resist saying that it is things that are unstable, and locate instability in her body. Yet you go on that she was not changing perspectives – so this does look like a very different case from the shamans, since (as I thought I understood you) it is their vision that changes, rather than their bodies that act to transform the objects they are seeing. Or is it the case that their bodies do change, and that causes the change in their vision?

A: I would say so. To'o's is a very special case of someone external to the shamanic universe observing a person, a very close one, in the process of change. I've never heard of any other case of this type of changing perspectives. For the mother, the blood was *chicha*, and that is why she was eager to drink it. The observing child saw maize *chicha* remains. I don't know what the mother herself saw. Probably maize *chicha* all the time. She, as a becoming jaguar, could not see otherwise, so I think that probably when she spat the maize, she had returned to the Wari' mode of body-perception. As I told you, it all depends on the specific case. It is as if they are always building their ontology-epistemology-cosmology. Could we say that? If so, is it an unstable ontology?

P: Drawing a deep breath and standing back. The term 'ontologies' may be unhelpful in that it would suggest to some (me included) that this is all-inclusive: we are dealing with a global account of what there is and we must expect such accounts to differ across different cultures. The Wari' (and others') ontology is contrasted with the Western one as if both were all-encompassing assumptions about the world. But in many of your examples I would say that more than one ontology is already in play *chez* the Wari'.

A: So, the above idea that they have one ontology, although one in a constant process of being made, a changing one, does not work for philosophy? I am a bit lost here.

P: It is not just that it does not work for philosophy (i.e. that philosophy is different). Rather more is at stake: what sense does it make to talk ontological talk here or in philosophy in the first place? The Wari' just get on with their lives, in which for them, corn is corn, *chicha* is *chicha*, with no problems (is that very unfair?). Perspectives kick in where different species or boundary-crossing individuals such as shamans are concerned. One consequence of that is the difficulty I raised about being versus becoming – a special Greek preoccupation for sure, but one where for the Wari' we have to say (don't we?) that 'the world' for them is both. There is stability and there is flux – but you comment that the latter is in the perspectives rather than in the things (insofar as they have an idea of 'things', where we have questioned the status of 'objects' before).

A: They have an idea of things, but they also know that different people see the things they (the Wari') see differently.

P: Of course, to capture that difference appeal is often made to 'ontology'. But I am increasingly wary of that move, just as I am of invoking 'incommensurability'. Okay, there is no neutral vocabulary in which to parse these different understandings, but that does not mean they are totally mutually unintelligible. This is one point where we need to subject many of our basic concepts to criticism and revision. One major problem is that 'ontology' began in philosophy, where it was used to talk about whatever exists as if that should be given a single all-encompassing answer. But that tends to leave no room whatsoever for multiple ontologies and so leads quickly to a swift dismissal of whatever does not chime with your own starting assumptions. But if 'one-world' solutions suffer from that flaw – we should learn to treat divergent views with more respect – 'multiple-world' ones owe the reader some account of their multiplicity.

A: Thank you for clarifying it for me. I am always at a loss when talking in terms of ontology. I never know how to phrase what I have experienced among the Wari'. One ontology? Multiple ontologies? What I know is that it is very different from my world here. Very different. That does not mean I cannot understand it if there is someone to explain it to me. Seeing my Wari' grandfather, the shaman-jaguar Orowam, acting strangely, as in the episode I mentioned before, when he began to see me and Abrão as prey, would be an incommensurable experience (I would say he was mad or ill) if there were not a kind person to explain to me that he was becoming a jaguar. With no translators, the perceptions would not be comprehensible and that could lead to awful experiences (like becoming prey, for example).

P: Now, some tactics used at this point seem to me unhelpful, even mystificatory. When we turn back to the data that prompts the many-worlds hypothesis, are we really dealing with multiple ontologies? Not in the sense of multiple 'everythings', for everything is by definition all-encompassing. 'Ontologies' designate a field of reality that is self-contained and all-embracing where that field is concerned. But what is a 'field of reality'? Is it something that is accessible to multiple observers or just to some group of them? We could say that fundamental particle physics implies an ontology that is actually accessed only by a very few, though in principle it is accessible to many. Wari' shamans following jaguars look to be a bit different in that that accessibility to non-shamans seems to be ruled out. But to talk of those shamans inhabiting a different world, a different reality, seems to conflict with the fact that they come back home. What about the Wari' as a whole? Again it seems to me that both 'ontology' and 'incommensurability' overdo the puzzles they present. For sure the puzzles warn us to suspend judgement if we are tempted to bring our usual assumptions to bear. But the price is a high one. We cannot judge by our standards: but the alternative seems to be to say that their standards are beyond reach.

A: It is complicated, isn't it? I am so relieved to know that you have some of the same questions as I do. Don't you think it all depends on our own relations? To whom are we trying to explain the Wari' way of being? Physicists? Anthropologists? To the Wari' themselves (like at school when the teacher asks them to talk about their 'cosmology' to the class of mixed ethnicities)? Could you and I convince someone in the academy that they are different from us if we do not use the term ontology?

P: On conceding that we are baffled, that's good honest methodology. But maybe there is a more fundamental lesson to be learned. I go on about the revisability of concepts. But their semantic stretch may suggest a far more radical philosophy of language and its limitations as a vehicle of communication, but at the same time offer a way ahead on some much-used – and abused – terminology. This is not the instability of your body or mine, but it is to promote the idea of a fundamental fluidity in the processes of understanding and communication. Definitions, in my view, so far from being helpful, even necessary, often get in the way.

A: I agree. So we are not looking for terminologies. But how to talk about things if we cannot systematize them? Will it be enough to say that the bodies are not unstable but that the world (including bodies) is in a constant flux, ever indeterminate? As if a whole world only crystalizes for a few moments, and then changes again. In Amazonia in general, the body (as a concept and as an object) is so central that it is useful to talk about unstable bodies in order to express their way of being. Doesn't it always depend on whom we are talking with? Amazonianists have a vocabulary and to speak with them you have to keep it; philosophers have another one. The point is that, after Philippe Descola and Eduardo Viveiros de Castro (following, of course, Lévi-Strauss himself), philosophical terminology got into Amazonian talk, and we cannot not use their terminology.

I understand that we (you and I) are trying here to escape it, finding new terms or no terms at all. Is that so?

P: You do a marvellous job of explaining the different Wari' world even without any recourse to 'ontology'. What does 'ontology' do to help? There's a problem in any case as to whether the multiplicity of ontologies is a matter of Wari' versus Western modernity, or one of multiple Wari' ontologies, and come to that of modern Western ones. What we are talking about ultimately is different experiences and ways of talking about those experiences – different values or senses of what is important, what people are expected to do in the face of disaster, sickness or death, what dangers they run if they do not get it right, what obligations they have to those they recognize as belonging to their group, or to others who do not. But we can do all of that without invoking ontologies as such.

A: I like the point that what varies is what people think is important. Like the importance of relations for many Indigenous peoples, which is above everything else. The focus of life is on doing relations, expanding or contracting them, depending on the situation, and doing the right things in each specific relational context. What you do here and now is not necessarily reproducible somewhere else, with someone else. All this Christian talk about the integrity of the self, the truthful self, is something that does not fit with the world they live in.

P: In modern urban industrialized societies the importance of relations (with kin, even with friends) tends to be dramatically downplayed – compared with the situation where 'family' meant a pretty widely extended group. Marilyn Strathern (2020) has made the point emphatically.

A: You are right, it is downplayed, but I think there is a reason for this, as the explicit discourse of Western urban people usually does not put relations in front. As Roy Wagner (2016) says, we strive to make culture, objects (books, technology, etc.), and we see relations as a private side of our lives, not the central meaning of it. Indians put relations in front, as the aim of all their lives, their actions.

P: You rightly go on to observe how complicated it is. But you yourself show how to illustrate differences by concrete examples, without going into ontologies. I recall that Tim Ingold (2021) is one who inveighs against theory in favour of concrete examples. You worry that we cannot get going to talk about things if we cannot systematize them. But systematizing runs the risk of doing less than justice to the changes in the subjects, the bodies, we are talking about.

A: Don't you think we are, in a way, trying to systematize otherwise, meaning that we are trying to find some more open categories, more fluid or less precise (like I found in Wari' maths)?

P: This is what insisting on 'semantic stretch' is all about. Obviously Amazonianists and philosophers each have their own vocabularies. But neither is set in stone. Our job is precisely to see where they will not do, where they need revision, even though our very revisions have to be expressed in a language that remains in touch with the original. Not 'no terms at all' and not necessarily coining new terms: rather, offering new understandings where all the concepts we use are subject to scrutiny as we make them fit (or fitter) for purpose.

A: Yes, I agree. Keeping in touch with the previous concepts is essential, even if we invert them, like Eduardo Viveiros de Castro did with the nature/culture pair to contrast naturalism and perspectivism. I have a very good example of it from my writings. In my first book (not translated into English – Vilaça 2017 [1992]), I realized that the Wari' concept of *jamixi'*, which nowadays I translate as 'double', was so different from our concept of soul that I decided to keep it in Wari' language, and repeat and repeat the word throughout the book. Of course I was young and naive and was trying to be faithful to Wari' experience. But in doing this their concept was kind of lost for discussion. Then I decided to explain it thoroughly and to translate it as 'double', which is also a term widely used by Amazonianists, but mainly when talking about shamans. I still feel very uncomfortable with both the 'soul' and 'double' translations, as for the Wari' it is something that a person does not have (as part of the body, for example), but might have in some circumstances. I was so naive at the beginning of my fieldwork that I asked them where their *jamixi'* was in their body, a crazy question that made them laugh and answer that they did not have a *jamixi'* (because, of course, they were healthy, not sick, not being kidnapped, not dreaming, not dying. In sum, they were not transforming at the moment they were talking with me).

P: I have no problems with leaving certain terms in transliteration rather than attempting to translate them, provided we give plenty of context on the range of uses. Chinese *qi* cannot be 'translated', nor even Greek *logos*.

A: Yes, but when you translate, people can use it in the semantic stretch mode. So, double or even soul become among the possible meanings of *jamixi'*.

P: Does not my use just now of 'sociological', 'philosophical', 'psychological' and the rest just show how far we are still trapped in a conceptual framework that reeks of its modernist and postmodernist origins? It is true that we continue to conduct these exchanges in English, even if it has gobbled up *qi* and *logos* and countless anthropological terms, such as Hau and Mana, by transliterating them. But the entire vocabulary we deploy should be understood to be in scare quotes: that's where semantic stretch kicks in and where we can insist on provisionality and revisability. To the objection that this leaves us in a morass of uncertainty and the threat of indefinite revisability, the answer should be that while the terminology is on the move, it still communicates. We make some progress in our investigation of how social relations impinge on ways of being in the world, on values and ideas of how to behave, how to flourish. But in the process we learn not just about divergent understandings of values, but how 'social relations' themselves are to be understood. We reach the conclusion that 'philosophy' has its part to play in helping to form answers to those key questions. But here too, in the process, what counts as 'philosophy' undergoes serious modification, with some parts of modern academic perceptions being downgraded, but other lessons from 'philosophy in the forest' contributing to our positive picture. And under 'psychology', do we not have to admit that we are still often at sea trying to understand consciousness, whatever vocabulary we conscript to help us? Whatever provisional answers we give, we surely recognize that they have radical implications for our understanding of humans' relations with other humans, with other animals, and with other sentient beings, if not also 'inanimate' ones (or whatever is to be thought of as such: note here some explicit scare quotes again).

If this leads to what might be thought the depressing conclusion that where we advance in understanding is more in understanding what remains to be understood than in grasping what we currently think we can understand, then so be it. But maybe we don't have to be quite as defensive as that. We can continue: we are not in a rush.

It would be wise, then, to concede that we just don't fully know – the good honest methodological point with which I began. But note that (a) this leaves us with no justification for any claim that 'we' (whoever) know better, and (b) even if we have to say we do not fully understand, that is no reason to say we have no purchase on any understanding whatsoever. It's hard work to be sure and faces multiple barriers to communication – translation not just between natural languages but within any given one – as we look to understand our interlocutors a bit better. I am not an ancient Greek, nor an ancient Chinese, but immersing myself in the texts (which are admittedly lacunose and biased), I eventually believe that I can get some inkling of what they are driving at, and even sometimes why.

We don't (I don't) choose ayahuasca as the route to inspiration (in life let alone in scholarship!). But we look for inspiration nevertheless when ourselves faced with life and death, and good and evil, and humans and other creatures. And what about the Gods? Who is going to deny the power of Aphrodite and of the Masters and Mistresses of the animals? We get a lot of inspiration from poetry and, yes, from science, at least on my view of science, which sees it as steeped in values and far closer to philosophy (of the non-academic sort) than is usually thought. Our poets have, alas, far less powerful political voices than they used to have, but we can and do still learn from them about the most minute as well as the grandest topics. The register in which ideas are communicated is so important, but that surely allows us to move from one register to another: as you do when you report on the Wari', thereby demonstrating the inspirations to be had not just from poetry and science but also from anthropology.

I don't doubt, however, that sometimes we are dealing with binary contrasts, but that is far rarer than generally used to be assumed in 'them and us' discussions. Often we are dealing with spectra, with continua. So analogously, not digital, but analogue. Of course it is hard work making such an analysis stick when we are dealing with groups, beliefs and practices that look different to the point of 'incommensurability'. But giving everyone their say is not impossible even if there is no neutral vocabulary in which to communicate.

A: Agreed, although I am always cautious to not lose sight of the differences, which could tell us a lot, at least for an anthropologist.

P: We have inherited a problem situation in which one way or another a stark contrast between 'them' (Indigenous peoples, ancients) and 'us' (supposedly enlightened scientific Westerners) holds sway. We can see many places where that is a travesty. Where we can find important differences, they may be in the styles of communication favoured or in particular items of belief or practice. The puzzlements cannot be denied (but then we are puzzling people ourselves). Our essential aim is to keep the possibility of understanding alive, even and especially where that may threaten some of our own cherished assumptions, where, as you know, one of my star examples is 'nature' itself.

A: I agree, but as I said above, communication of course implies misunderstandings, and paying attention to them can teach us even more, perhaps, than looking at the similarities. See the Wari' paying attention to details of strangeness when they meet a jaguar-person, for example. If they focus on communication, which in fact happens, they will be dead (meaning, they will become a jaguar).

P: Many aspects of human behaviour, to other humans, other animals and the environment, in human history do not add up to a pretty picture. But the effort to understand better is a liberating experience. That effort has repeatedly been thwarted by laziness, greed and selfishness. But that is no reason to give up. The optimist in me serves up reminders of how amazing our sociality can be, even if the pessimist so often has to admit to some dismay.

Stimulated by the problems of understanding widely divergent views of what there is in different ancient (as well as modern) cultures, I often talk about the multidimensionality of reality, which does of course allow multiple perspectives on it while keeping them within reach of one another (they should not be thought to be totally mutually unintelligible, even though there is no totally neutral, innocent vocabulary to talk about them).

A: I am not totally sure about that. Regarding the Wari', we could say that if it were not for the translator-shamans, the multiple realities would not be mutually intelligible, with serious consequences, like disease and death (if you were to drink jaguar's blood, wrongly taking it for *chicha*). So, people have to listen to these accounts of kidnapping, shamanism, diseases, to learn how to translate in case they are kept when alone in the forest. The Wari' could say (they never did, but I guess they could) that as an anthropologist, I could learn a lot about their social life, but would not be able to circulate freely, with no danger, if I did not know all the possibilities of transformation and disease. Even if I knew, I could have become ill, kidnapped or hurt.

CHAPTER 15

Anthropologists and Philosophers

P: The importance of not losing sight of differences prompts me to wonder how our own distinctive backgrounds, yours and mine, are playing out in our discussion. You the anthropologist insist on the distinctiveness of the materials you uncover in your fieldwork, the strangeness included. As an ancient philosopher originally, I learned to be very wary of the supposed alienness of those who were labelled barbarians by ancients or moderns when that was used as an excuse to downgrade them, even to the point of claiming they were irrational (though for some modern scholars an important motive in that downgrading was to upgrade the Greeks, or some of them at least, as 'rational' and 'enlightened' 'like us'). That has often led me to turn the tables: we are still alien ourselves, not just in our crazy customs and beliefs, but in the pride and joy (for some) of high science and philosophy. Our 'enlightenment' can be full of darkness.

A: You are right, we are aiming at different points. If I were in the 1960s or before, I would have to be much more focused on showing their rationality (like Lévi-Strauss 1966 does in the science of the concrete, and Evans-Pritchard 1956 on the Nuer). Now that they have their human status guaranteed (at least regarding anthropologists), I can focus on the differences. I am not making any judgement on barbarism, and I agree with you that we who live in modern urbanized societies are the barbarians, not 'they', the others who don't. I am totally convinced of it by now.

P: In a funny way, for modern ancient philosophers to immerse themselves in ancient philosophy, to the point of thinking like a Plato or an Aristotle, would be to become dead too, not by transforming into a jaguar, but by losing sight precisely of those differences that we have just been speaking about.

I am intrigued by what I see as a kind of complementarity emerging between the two of us (cf. my remarks about backgrounds). I am all for breaking down barriers and seeing us all (ancients and moderns, more or less literate and institutionalized) in remarkably similar boats in the final analysis – for all the differences that we both recognize, and that you insist on, in just how we get along with coping with dreams and death and illness and trying to understand them and one another. I might see myself as trying to transform into … an anthropologist. You are observing and sympathizing (and succeeding in being an anthropologist where I am only trying), but at the same time keeping your distance even while you have multiple Wari' fathers and mothers and brothers and sisters, for all the world as any fearless Wari' would.

A: Several points of our discussion are due to different focus or interests: as a philosopher, you want to apply your notion of semantic stretch to 'humanity'. As an anthropologist I aim at 'humanities' (plural) and fear that ignoring that plurality would lead me to lose the main points that the Indigenous people themselves are trying to teach me. If the Wari' say they are like this (meaning speak their language, think like this, have darker skins, like eating worms, etc.) because their body is different from ours, and that because of this we see different things, why should I try to compare the similarities and not focus on the differences? Each of us is pushing the thread in one direction and that is what I think is really interesting in our metalogues. We both agree with each other, but then we say: but what if it is …

P: The philosophers of science would say that there are no unvarnished facts, if unvarnished means theory-free, for as I said before, all come with some conceptual framework (and that is certainly true, and especially so of the most fancy theoretical physics or cosmology or genetics). Conversely, philosophers of language register that 'metaphors' are difficult to pin down (I do without them by substituting 'semantic stretch'). But my inspiration from anthropology is strengthened, not weakened, by those two points. I am not (laughably) presupposing that anthropologists are writing poetry. But that does not prevent me from registering sometimes – in the best ethnography, quite often – that the lives the anthropologists are introducing me to are full of the poetic – and not just when Philippe Descola (2013) describes the Achuar women singing to their plants in their gardens.

Anthropologists should relax: the world is not to be reduced to what is considered 'scientific'. And scientists don't always exhibit speech and behaviour that meet the norms popularly associated with science. Semantic stretch itself stretches over both 'facts' and images (or 'metaphors').

A: We have complementary views. You have an interest in the similarities, as all differences contribute to a more complex view of human beings. I am more interested in the differences and how they relate – as for example in my work about conversion to Christianity (Vilaça 2016). It was only possible to understand how they experienced it by focusing on the differences between the Wari' and the missionaries and on how the translations of key Christian concepts are done differently by one or the other. It wouldn't have worked if I had focused on the coincidences as what allowed them to relate. In a way, of course they existed, but they were more in the missionaries' view (all God's children, the lost people from Israel, etc.) than on the Wari' side. In fact, it is all about where you want to get to.

P: We deal with different source material that poses distinct problems, though they all have in common the attempt to understand. We respond to what others have had to say, wrestling with the problems, and that includes registering, as we have done, how unsatisfactory we feel certain fashionable suggestions are. At the same time we have to admit, and do admit, to remaining baffled. We sense the opportunity to learn from these puzzling encounters, and certainly can undertake some basic revisions in our own assumptions about personhood, agency, relationships and bodies, and then also about communication and understanding themselves. The very possibility of identifying mistranslations reminds us that they can sometimes be avoided. What we endeavour to work towards, however tentatively, is to make the most of our complementarity. The goal could be described as a (more) philosophical anthropology and a (more) anthropological philosophy. We do not underestimate the further work that remains to be done.

Conclusion

Every society has some more or less extensive, more or less successful means to survive, even while many do not in the long run. The technology and the social institutions needed and used vary appreciably. Surviving in the Amazonian rainforest requires different skills from those of Pacific navigators. Those who set out to explore the Northwest Passage perished when crossing terrain where Inuit had lived and flourished for many centuries. We pride ourselves in modern industrial society on having technologies that are vastly superior to those of our predecessors. Yet those technologies have not made the world a safer place. Quite the reverse. With still-uncontrolled climate change we run the risk of destroying the environment on which every living thing depends. While we succeeded in developing vaccines against COVID-19, that is not the last pandemic that humans will ever face. And death, for sure, finishes us all.

The human predicament is universal. Yet there are enormous differences in how different peoples respond to the difficulties and dangers, not just of disease and of death, but of dealing with our fellows in our own societies and in others. Those differences pose two kinds of problems. The first is that of understanding others, the second that of learning from them. Baffled as we are by the strange beliefs and practices we see around us, how can we begin to understand their basis and rationale – and do they indeed have one? Then, secondly, what can we learn from them to improve our own prospects of flourishing? We must bear in mind that most societies have assumed that there is nothing much to learn from others and that they themselves have the best answers to the problems. It would be foolish to fall into the same trap ourselves.

Human historiography has been monopolized by the victors, who have all too often dismissed other peoples' beliefs as worthless. In the most recent rise of modern Western hegemonic imperialism, science has been the watchword to justify the victors' claims to superiority and to pinpoint the shortcomings of the vanquished. We have the truth, or much of it anyway, secured by rational methods of investigation. Earlier or alternative belief systems can safely be dismissed as fantasy, myth or superstition. Armed with better weaponry and as the carriers of new diseases (as Diamond 1997 emphasized), Westerners expanded throughout the twentieth century and only at its very end have been challenged effectively by Asian powers. Meanwhile, so-called primitive societies have been declining or quite simply disappearing at an exponential rate.

But students of ancient societies and ethnographers of existing ones are not just there to record the catastrophic effects of these Western developments. It is not just a question of telling it how it happened, *wie es eigentlich gewesen*. Our vital task is, rather, to learn from others. Where missionaries have set about converting others to bring them to a totally new point of view, we should grasp the opportunity to have those others teach us a thing or two, to remind us in the first instance of the multiple ways in which humans may flourish.

This is the principle that has guided our explorations here.

The Wari', the ancient Greeks and Chinese, and many other peoples give us access to some very strange ideas and practices, and we have endeavoured to make the most of that. In grappling with problems of translation we have often had to register the limits of translatability, charting differences in the conceptual schemes themselves in which what nevertheless passes as common knowledge is cast. We learn that for the Wari' the term *kwerexi'*, which we may translate as 'body', also covers 'behaviour', 'feelings', 'manners' and 'intelligence'. For the Chinese, *qi* means both 'breath' and 'energy', and many other things. But instead of concluding that these native expressions were category mistakes, we have rather to revise our own categories, recognizing that our own standard way of establishing the boundaries between them is not the only possible one.

The temptation sometimes used to be to reject pretty well everything found alien as error, superstition, irrational, wrong-headed, perverse or whatever. But that was based, of course, on the assumption that we had understood the strange ideas and practices in question in the first place. Further investigation and reflection often reveal that we have overestimated our ability to interpret what is going on, leading to the sobering realization that we have been severely underestimating the difficulties of doing so. Now, that can and often has led to an extreme reaction in the opposite direction – to the conclusion that strictly speaking, all these alien systems are unintelligible to outsiders. To understand the ancient Greeks you have to become an ancient Greek, which of course you cannot. You need to marry a Wari' to achieve *iri' Wari'* status.

Nevertheless, we embarked on this exercise sharing the conviction that some understanding is possible, despite all the strangeness of the material we are trying to come to terms with, from whatever period or society that material comes. But what understanding have we actually achieved? Time and again the questions relate to ideas about what really exists, about who to count as fellow human beings, about how to cope with life – and death and disease – and about values. So it is as well to remind ourselves that we are still often at a loss as to the answers to such questions, even if we can see that some of them cannot in any case be given 'straight' answers (philosophers used to get very excited about diagnosing phony, i.e. purely linguistic, philosophical problems: with a wave of a clarificatory wand they decreed that there was no problem there at all). Yet those remaining doubts should be no excuse simply to admit defeat, but rather a stimulus for the pursuit of new possibilities of understanding.

It is true that where modern theoretical physics and cosmology and biology are concerned, we can say that many discoveries have been made, and we can identify certain errors (including modern ones) as just that. At the same time we have to recognize that such scientific questions are not the most immediate concerns of ordinary folk in the streets of London or the clearings in the Amazonian forest. Those concerns are to do with coping with human relations, interacting with other living beings and with the environment, how to make a living, let alone ensure human flourishing, what values to hold dear, and so on. To cope with those we humans not only need science: we need empathy and understanding. This is, we hope, where our combination of anthropologizing and philosophizing can help.

The two of us bring our own presumptions and values to the table, for sure – most, but not all, of which we have to be prepared to revise, and some to abandon. When we encounter writers endorsing slavery or excluding people from 'humanity' on the grounds that they talk or dress in a funny way, we dissent, even while we are obliged to investigate why those writers took or take those views. But more fruitfully, when we see how a different and more respectful attitude to non-humans, or the environment, or simply the strange and unfamiliar is adopted, we have the chance to learn.

The multitude of ways of being in the world serves then as a reminder of our own lack of imagination, or certainly of its limits. The two of us are not in business endorsing, *per impossibile*, any and every idea or system of beliefs that our evidence throws up. But even the most puzzling ones are food for thought, perhaps especially the most puzzling ones. Are we just dreaming? No. But asking that question reminds us how little we know about consciousness, among ourselves and, it could be, among butterflies and jaguars.

References

Barth, Fredrik. 1975. *Ritual and Knowledge among the Baktaman of New Guinea.* New Haven, CT: Yale University Press.
Basso, Ellen B. 1987. *In Favor of Deceit: A Study of Tricksters in an Amazonian Society.* Tucson, AZ: University of Arizona Press.
Bateson, Gregory. 1972. *Steps to an Ecology of Mind.* San Francisco: Chandler.
Behr, Charles Allison. 1968. *Aelius Aristides and the Sacred Tales.* Amsterdam: Hakkert.
Burkert, Walter. 1972. *Lore and Science in Ancient Pythagoreanism.* Cambridge, MA: Harvard University Press.
Descola, Philippe. [2005] 2013. *Beyond Nature and Culture*, trans. J. Lloyd. Chicago: Chicago University Press.
Diamond, Jared. 1997. *Guns, Germs and Steel.* New York: Norton.
Diels, Hermann, and Walter Kranz (eds). 1952. *Die Fragmente der Vorsokratiker*, 3 vols., 6th edn. Berlin: Weidmann.
Dodds, Eric R. 1951. *The Greeks and the Irrational.* Berkeley: University of California Press.
Evans-Pritchard, E.E. 1937. *Witchcraft Oracles and Magic among the Azande.* Oxford: Clarendon Press.
———. 1956. *Nuer Religion.* Oxford: Clarendon Press.
Goody, Jack. 1977. *The Domestication of the Savage Mind.* Cambridge: Cambridge University Press.
Graham, Angus C. 1981. *Disputers of the Tao.* La Salle, IL: Open Court.
Guthrie, W.K.C. 1969. *A History of Greek Philosophy: Volume 3, The Fifth-Century Enlightenment.* Cambridge: Cambridge University Press.
Hsu, Elisabeth. 2010. *Pulse Diagnosis in Early Chinese Medicine: The Telling Touch.* Cambridge: Cambridge University Press.
Hughes, Ted. 1972. *Crow.* London: Faber and Faber.

Ingold, Tim. 2021. *The Perception of the Environment.* (1st edn 2000) London: Routledge.
Kafka, Franz. 1935. *Die Verwandlung.* Frankfurt am Main: Suhrkamp.
Kahn, Charles H. 1973. *The Verb 'Be' in Ancient Greek.* Dordrecht: Reidel.
Kopenawa, Davi, and Bruce Albert. 2013. *The Falling Sky: Words of a Yanomami Shaman*, trans. Nicholas Elliott and Alison Dundy. Cambridge, MA: Harvard University Press.
Latour, Bruno. [1991] 1993. *We Have Never Been Modern*, trans. C. Porter. Cambridge, MA: Harvard University Press.
Lévi-Strauss, Claude. [1962] 1966. *The Savage Mind*, trans. anon. London: Weidenfeld and Nicholson.
———. [1958] 1968. *Structural Anthropology*, trans. C. Jacobson and B.G. Schoepf. New York: Basic Books.
———. [1964–71] 1970–81. *Introduction to the Science of Mythology*, 4 vols, trans. J. and D. Weightman. London: Jonathan Cape.
———. 2013. *The Other Face of the Moon*, trans. J.M. Todd. Cambridge, MA: Harvard University Press.
Lloyd, G.E.R. 1966. *Adversaries and Authorities.* Cambridge: Cambridge University Press.
———. 2007. '*Pneuma* between Body and Soul', *Journal of the Royal Anthropological Society* 13: S135–46.
Lloyd, G.E.R., and Nathan Sivin. 2002. *The Way and the Word.* New Haven, CT: Yale University Press.
Major, John S. 1993. *Heaven and Earth in Early Han Thought.* Albany: State University of New York Press.
Mynott, Jeremy. 2018. *Birds in the Ancient World.* Oxford: Oxford University Press.
Parker, Robert. 1983. *Miasma: Pollution and Purification in Early Greek Religion.* Oxford: Clarendon Press.
Sivin, Nathan. 1995. 'State, Cosmos and Body in the Last Three Centuries B.C.', *Harvard Journal of Asiatic Studies* 55: 5–37.
Sommer, Deborah. 2008. 'Boundaries of the Ti Body', *Asia Major* 21(1): 293–304.
Sterckx, Roel. 2000. 'Transforming the Beasts: Animals and Music in Early China', *T'oung Pao* 86: 1–46.
Strathern, Marilyn. 2020. *Relations: An Anthropological Account.* Durham, NC: Duke University Press.
Vilaça, Aparecida. 2016. *Praying and Preying: Christianity in Indigenous Amazonia.* Oakland: University of California Press.
———. 2017. *Comendo como gente: Formas do canibalismo wari' (Pakaa Nova).* (1st edn 1992) Rio de Janeiro: Mauad X.

———. 2018. 'The Devil and the Secret Life of Numbers', *HAU: Journal of Ethnographic Theory* 8(1–2): 6–19.
———. 2021a. 'A Pagan Arithmetic: Unstable Sets in Indigenous Amazonia', *Interdisciplinary Science Reviews* 46(3): 304–24.
———. 2021b. *Paletó and Me: Memories of My Indigenous Father.* Stanford, CA: Stanford University Press.
Viveiros de Castro, Eduardo. 1998. 'Cosmological Deixis and Amerindian Perspectivism', *Journal of the Royal Anthropological Institute* 4(3): 469–88.
———. 2004. 'Perspectival Anthropology and the Method of Controlled Equivocation', *Tipití: Journal of the Society for the Anthropology of Lowland South America* 2(1): 3–22.
———. [2009] 2014. *Cannibal Metaphysics*, trans. P. Skafish. Minneapolis, MN: Univocal.
———. 2015. *The Relative Native: Essays on Indigenous Conceptual Worlds.* Chicago: University of Chicago Press.
Wagner, Roy. 2016. *The Invention of Culture.* 2nd edn (1st edn 1975). Chicago: University of Chicago Press.
Williams, Bernard. 2002. *Truth and Truthfulness.* Princeton, NJ: Princeton University Press.

Index

abduction, 4, 8, 10–11, 17, 33, 38, 41, 94
abnormal, 18, 22
Achuar, 108
accountability, 69
agency, 34, 41, 60–61, 80, 109
agoutis, 38
alternation, 57–58, 92
anaconda, 49, 66
antibiotics, 72, 82
appearances, 34, 65, 69
Archimedes, 28–29
Aristides, Aelius, 29–30
Aristotle, 15–16, 29, 62, 107
arithmetic, 51
Asclepius, 29
astronomy, 24
authority, 28, 46, 71–72, 85, 91
authorship, 20
axioms, 83
ayahuasca, 49, 103
Azande, 84

Baktaman, 78
barbarians, 106–7
Barth, Fredrik, 78
Bateson, Gregory, 5, 87
beans, 24–25
becoming, 37–40, 44, 91–93, 96
being, 91–93, 96, 98
belief, 1, 3–4, 23–24, 26–27, 80, 82, 86, 103–4, 106, 110–11, 113
believing, 73, 80, 82, 87, 103
Bible, 1, 86
biology, 27–8, 113
blood, 7–9, 32–35, 37, 40–41, 44–45, 48–50, 59, 80, 92–95, 105
Buddhism, 20
butterflies, 13–16, 20, 88, 114

categories, 19, 26, 46, 75, 100, 112
causality, 21, 23–24, 70
challenge, 4, 10, 13, 16, 26, 30, 69, 71, 84, 111
charlatans, 23–24
charms, 26, 29
children, 3, 22, 79, 83, 86–87, 93
Christianity, 1, 23, 50, 71, 73–75, 80–82, 87, 89, 99, 108
climate, 61, 110
commensality, 8
communication, 6, 13, 49, 98, 103–4, 109
competitiveness, 69, 82

consciousness, 27, 102, 114
contexts, 4, 36, 43, 76, 78–79, 84, 86–87, 99, 101
conversion, 1, 18, 37, 73, 82, 108, 111
cosmogony, 62
cosmology, 2, 25, 62, 95, 98, 108, 113
counterintuitiveness, 2, 4
courage, 20
courts, 84, 87
culture, 7, 59, 63, 69, 100
cunning, 20, 78
cure, 9, 24, 30, 41, 53, 70, 72, 82
curiosity, 12

Daoism, 13
death, 1–2, 15, 41, 67, 73–74, 79, 89, 92, 99, 103, 105, 107, 110, 112
deceit, 20, 69–72, 77–78, 89
deduction, 82, 83, 90
definition, 44, 60, 81, 97–98
demons, 23
demonstration, 83. *See also* proof
Descola, Philippe, 55, 98, 108
determinism, linguistic, 39
devil, 71, 73, 87
disease, 1–2, 18, 21, 23–4, 26, 29, 54, 56, 60–61, 70, 82, 89, 99, 105, 110–12
Dodds, Eric R, 24
doubles, 8, 14–15, 32–33, 35–36, 38, 42–3, 54, 56, 58, 65, 69, 71, 88, 101
dreaming, 12–14, 20, 22, 36, 89, 101, 107, 114

eclipse, 24
edibility, 11, 12, 18–19, 44, 58, 66
efficacy, 30
elements, 25, 62–63

Empedocles, 21, 24–29
empirical, 21
enemies, 37, 39, 72, 75, 79, 90
Enlightenment, 24, 106
environment, 90, 104, 110, 113
epistemology, 56, 91, 95
equivalents, 35–36, 48–53
essence, 16, 51
Euclid, 29
Evans-Pritchard, E.E., 84, 106
evidence, 2–3, 24–25, 27–29, 44, 83, 113
evolution, 27
existence, 44, 51, 60, 74
experience, 1, 3–4, 27, 34, 46, 50, 54, 66, 69, 72, 74, 78, 87, 90, 93, 97, 99, 101, 104
experts, 23
explanation, 21, 29, 45, 47

faith, 4, 29
fakes, 19, 40, 43, 68, 70, 76
fear, 8, 22
feelings, 11, 27, 42, 44, 50, 112
felicity, 30
fiction, 23, 78, 88–89
fish, 7, 9, 18, 26, 37, 51, 66, 74–75
fishermen, 16, 21
folk-tales, 21
function, 16, 62
fur, 8, 10, 33–34, 41, 44, 57, 59

Galileo, 28
Genesis, 18
genius, 28
geometry, 63
God, 18, 23, 25–26, 29–30, 73–74, 82, 86, 103, 109
Goody, Jack, 84–5
Graham, Angus C., 13–14
gullibility, 3, 23, 70, 84

hallucinations, 12, 14, 36
healing, 26, 35, 42, 54, 69, 71, 82. *See also* cure
heart, 11, 42, 44, 62, 65
Heraclitus, 24, 61, 92
hierarchy, 67
Hippocratic writings, 26, 29, 69
Homer, 15. *See also Odyssey*
Huainanzi, 12, 62
humanity, 2, 6, 15, 59, 66, 107, 113
humans, 2–4, 6–7, 10–11, 13–15, 18–21, 26, 28, 32, 35, 37–38, 40–43, 46, 48–9, 52, 56, 58–59, 65–66, 71, 75, 82, 94, 103–4, 106–8, 112–13
hunting, 11, 32, 42, 46–47, 52, 54, 75, 85, 87, 92
hybrids, 27, 34, 36

identity, 20, 32, 51, 58
imagination, 4, 90, 113
imperialism, 111
incantations, 26, 29
incommensurability, 96–97, 103
incompatibility, 25, 82
inconsistency, 81
incontrovertibility, 76, 83
Ingold, Tim, 100
initiation, 52, 78
intelligence, 11, 42–45, 65, 78, 112
intentionality, 77
Inuit, 110

Japan, 63–64

Kafka, Franz, 88–89
Kepler, Johannes, 28
kidnapping, 7, 42–43, 45, 49–50, 56–59, 65–66, 68, 89, 101, 105
kin, 7–8, 10–11, 12, 27, 32, 34, 38–39, 43, 47, 49, 68, 92, 99

knowledge, 16, 28, 50, 66, 69, 74, 76, 78, 82, 91–92, 94, 112
Kopenawa, Davi, 50

language, 6–7, 39, 46, 51, 55–56, 59, 85, 87, 91, 98, 100, 103, 107–8
Latour, Bruno, 22
Lévi-Strauss, Claude, 21, 49, 63–64, 70, 84, 98, 106
lies, 70, 73, 76–77, 87
literacy, 2, 20–21, 29, 69, 85–86, 107
logos, 23, 101

madness, 2, 97
magic, 17, 24–26, 28, 70
mathematics, 24, 63, 83, 85, 100
medicine, 26, 30, 83
  temple, 29–30
mentality, 3, 84
metamorphosis, 16, 42, 57, 88
metaphor, 3, 17, 19, 108
metempsychosis, 24
methodology, 25, 28, 98
mind, 4, 11, 77, 89
miracle, 17, 80–81
  Greek, 28
missionaries, 1, 18, 37, 73–74, 82, 108–9, 111
monkeys, 8, 17–18, 32–34, 38, 53
  spider monkey, 18–19, 65–66
morality, 3, 11, 21, 62, 71, 76–78, 90
multidimensionality, 104
Mynott, Jeremy, 15
myth, 3, 12, 18, 21–2, 23, 49–50, 59, 66, 74, 77, 79, 86, 89–90, 110

nature, 4, 7, 12, 16, 17, 23, 26, 28, 100, 104
Newton, Isaac, 28

objectivity, 60, 89
objects, 42, 55–56, 94, 96, 98, 100
observation, 12, 16, 94, 97
Odyssey, 78
ontology, 37, 55–56, 63, 89, 91, 93–100
oracle, 26
orality, 2, 20–1, 69, 85–86

paca, 7, 50, 92
paradigms, 20
paradox, 3–4
peccary, 17–18, 52–53, 92
perception, 32–33, 41, 58, 60, 91, 93–5
personhood, 8, 34, 36, 38, 41–44, 47, 49, 52, 56–57, 66, 86, 93–94, 104, 109
perspectives, 6–7, 20, 30, 32–35, 38, 42–43, 45, 48–49, 52, 54, 55–58, 68, 71, 81, 92–96, 100, 105
perspectivism, 6, 93, 100, 107
persuasion, 25
Plato, 21, 29, 63, 83, 107
play, 19, 32, 71, 73, 79
pluralism, 84
pneuma, 62
poetry, 28, 88, 90, 103, 108
positivism, 24, 28–29
predators, 6–7, 47, 66
predication, 48, 51
prey, 6–8, 18–20, 35, 40–41, 44, 46–47, 56, 58, 66, 75, 97
process, 36, 40, 60, 63, 92, 95
progress, 3, 23, 28, 30
proof, 72, 74, 76, 83, 87, 89–90
propositions, 76
provisionality, 77, 102
psychiatry, 30
psychoanalysis, 68

psychology, 30, 101–2
purifiers, 26, 29
Purifications, 26
Pythagoras, 24–27
Pythagoreans, 24, 67

Qi, 61–63, 101, 112
Quesalid, 70, 84

rationality, 23, 29–30, 106, 111
reality, 14, 40, 43, 60, 81, 87, 89–90, 97, 105, 112
reason, 23, 28–29, 91
registers, 15, 74, 81, 87, 89, 103
relations, 20, 32, 40–43, 60, 71–73, 75, 90, 99–100, 102, 109, 113
relatives, 7, 34, 36, 43–44, 49, 53, 56, 58, 85, 92 (*see also* kin)
religion, 4, 24, 26, 81–82
revelation, 84
reversibility, 27, 66
revision, 61, 77, 96, 98, 100, 102, 109, 112–13
rituals, 6, 13, 24–25, 28, 71, 87
rivalry, 69–70
rulers, 13, 62

sages, 25, 62, 73, 76
scepticism, 84–5
school, 86, 98
science, 4, 21, 24–30, 76–77, 81–82, 83, 90, 103, 106, 108, 111, 113
scrutiny, 29, 100
semantic stretch, 45, 100–102, 107–8
sentience, 2, 27, 102
shamans, 1, 6–7, 9, 17, 19–20, 24, 32, 35–36, 38, 41–42, 46, 52–53, 54, 56–57, 60, 65–66, 69–75, 81–82, 92–97, 101, 105

sickness, 40–41, 52–53, 54, 60, 69–71, 99, 101. *See also* disease
Sivin, Nathan, 61
skills, 29, 42, 72, 86, 110
snakes, 13, 18–19
solids, 63
sorcery, 73
soul, 4, 8, 15, 24, 26, 42–44, 67, 101
species, 7, 16, 17–18, 24, 27, 52, 96
speech acts, 13
spirits, 8, 43, 73
stability, 38, 54, 61, 64, 65, 68, 78–79, 88, 93–94, 96
stars, 29
Sterckx, Roel, 62
Strathern, Marilyn, 99
Stoics, 62, 92
structuralism, 21
styles, 26, 30, 84, 104
substances, 63
superstition, 23, 25–26, 30, 84, 111–12
survival, 68, 70, 110

taboos, 19, 78
tapirs, 7, 11, 17, 48, 50, 53, 55, 58, 92
technology, 82, 100, 110
Thales, 24–25, 28–29
theology, 83
Theophrastus, 16
theory-laden, 16
therapy, 30, 52, 62
tradition, 1, 24, 28, 84
transformations, 3–4, 9, 12, 14–15, 17–20, 22, 27, 32–47, 52–53, 55–57, 59–62, 65–67, 69, 80, 86–87, 88, 91–95, 101, 107
transgressions, 21
translation, 4, 9, 33, 35–36, 42–43, 45, 48, 52, 55, 61, 73, 77, 91–2, 97, 101, 103, 105, 108, 111–12
transmigration, 67
transubstantiation, 80–1
true/false, 18, 28, 39–41, 72–8, 82, 84, 89
trust, 72, 75, 82, 83, 92
truthfulness, 83–84, 89, 99

understanding, 3–5, 13, 19, 26, 42, 44, 49, 73, 84, 88, 90, 96–98, 100, 102–4, 107, 109, 110, 112–13

validity, 25, 83
values, 21, 79, 90, 99, 102–3, 112–13
veracity, 10, 71, 90
verification, 76, 81
vision, 1, 7, 34, 36, 38–39, 41, 50, 54, 56–57, 60, 65, 70–71, 75, 92, 94–96
Viveiros de Castro, Eduardo, 7, 32, 55, 94, 98, 100
voting, 25

Wagner, Roy, 100
warfare, 1, 19, 75
warriors, 72, 85
wild, 16, 27, 52
Williams, Bernard, 83–84, 89
witches, 18, 73, 84
words, 9, 23, 26, 30, 36
worlds, 2, 7, 15, 32, 55, 73–74, 81–82, 89, 91, 93–94, 96–97

Xenophanes, 24

Yanomami, 76–7
yin/yang, 61

Zhuangzi, 13–14, 20, 61, 68, 88

www.ingramcontent.com/pod-product-compliance
Lightning Source LLC
Chambersburg PA
CBHW060032040426
42333CB00042B/2313